Theatre Artisans and Their Craft

Theatre Artisans and Their Craft: The Allied Arts Fields profiles fourteen remarkable artists and technicians who elevate theatre production to new dimensions, explore new materials and technologies, and introduce new safety standards and solutions.

Readers will learn how the featured artists delved into entrepreneurial ventures and created their own work for themselves; researching, studying, and experimenting, seeking answers when none were available. The book explores how to make an impact in the entertainment industry from behind the scenes, and how students can model themselves after these successful professionals to jump-start their career in theatre production.

Aimed at theatre and film practitioners in the allied arts fields, *Theatre Artisans and Their Craft* offers a collection of success stories that are both inspiring and informative.

Rafael Jaen is a costume designer, educator, and author. He is Associate Professor and Chair of the Department of Performing Arts at the University of Massachusetts Boston. He is the Vice-President for Communications at the United States Institute for Theatre Technology (USITT).

Holly Poe Durbin is a costume designer, educator, and author. She heads the Costume Design program at the University of California, Irvine. She is President of the University/Resident Theatre Association (URTA) and a member of the Publications Committee at the United States Institute for Theatre Technology (USITT).

Christin Essin is Associate Professor of Theatre History at Vanderbilt University in Nashville, Tennessee. She is a member of the Publications Committee at the United States Institute for Theatre Technology (USITT).

BACKSTAGE

Series Editor: Rafael Jaen

Backstage is the result of a publishing partnership between USITT and Routledge. The series consists of books that focus on the various aspects of the technical theatre industry. It celebrates the professionals that make theatre happen in the shops, backstage, and every other corner of this field.

Theatre Artisans and Their Craft
The Allied Arts Fields
Edited by Rafael Jaen, Holly Poe Durbin, and Christin Essin

For more information about this series, please visit: https://www.routledge.com/series/USITT

Theatre Artisans and Their Craft

The Allied Arts Fields

Edited by Rafael Jaen, Holly Poe Durbin, and Christin Essin

Routledge
Taylor & Francis Group
NEW YORK AND LONDON

A co-publication of Routledge and USITT.

First published 2020
by Routledge
52 Vanderbilt Avenue, New York, NY 10017

and by Routledge
2 Park Square, Milton Park, Abingdon, Oxon, OX14 4RN

Routledge is an imprint of the Taylor & Francis Group, an informa business

Library of Congress Cataloging-in-Publication Data
Names: Jaen, Rafael, editor. | Durbin, Holly Poe, 1957– editor. | Essin, Christin, editor.
Title: Theatre artisans and their craft : the allied arts fields / edited by Rafael Jaen, Holly Poe Durbin, and Christin Essin.
Description: New York, NY : Routledge, 2020. | Series: Backstage | Includes index.
Identifiers: LCCN 2019016947 | ISBN 9780815352211 (hardback ; alk. paper) |
ISBN 9780815352228 (paperback ; alk. paper) | ISBN 9781351131070 (ebook)
Subjects: LCSH: Set designers—United States—Interviews. | Theaters—Stage-setting and scenery.
Classification: LCC PN2096.A1 T476 2020 | DDC 792.02/5092273 [B]—dc23
LC record available at https://lccn.loc.gov/2019016947

ISBN: 978-0-8153-5221-1 (hbk)
ISBN: 978-0-8153-5222-8 (pbk)
ISBN: 978-1-351-13107-0 (ebk)

Typeset in Gill Sans and Avenir
by Apex CoVantage LLC
Printed in Canada

This book is dedicated to the guilds of craftspeople making backstage magic in live theatre, TV, and film.

CONTENTS

FOREWORD

The idea for this book was born at a Kennedy Center American College Theatre Festival (KCACTF) six years ago. After showing a jaw-dropping art portfolio, the owner, an art student from a community college, told me that he didn't think that he had a future in the theatre arts because it wasn't his major. Luckily, prop master Jay Duckworth (who is featured in one of this book's chapters) was attending the same festival, and after seeing the work ended up offering a summer internship to the student to join him during the summer at the Public Theatre in New York City. What got my attention, at the time, was that the student did not realize that it takes a village to produce effective storytelling, and that many allied arts translate effectively to the needs of a theatre or screen production.

Later, as I started the research for the potential book, I came across a group of like-minded individuals at the United States Institute for Theatre Technology (USITT) Publications Committee who believed in the project. The journey included compiling a list of names of about two hundred theatre artists, and we agreed that the pool of writers would consist of experienced authors alongside folks who had never written before, and that they would get mentoring along the way. We had so much material that it made sense to agree to a three-book series (to start with) focusing on the work of craftspeople, management folks, technical directors, and more. Finally, FOCAL Press accepted the proposal, and two distinguished co-editors, Holly Poe Durbin and Christin Essin, joined me. We juggled busy schedules with numerous professional engagements and demanding academic calendars, staying inspired by the writers' efforts and what we learned about the subjects that they chose from the master list.

This collection of masters presents several ways to create an impact in entertainment from "behind the scenes." Some followed a formal path, studying their subject in college. Others followed a guild model, apprenticing with masters in their field. One forged a journey that led from Renaissance fairs and cosplay to the online forum DeviantArt. They come from all over: North Carolina, Oregon, Texas, Wisconsin, England, and many other places. They've made careers around the country as well: New York, Portland, Santa Fe, Washington DC, and Houston, to mention just a few. Some became entrepreneurs, running their own creative businesses, and some combine regular employment with a freelance career.

What do these artists have in common? They all combine exceptional artistry with technical skills. Recognizing that formal education cannot always teach mastery of handcrafts, they added personal research and practice to expand their knowledge. They all experimented with materials, diving in to explore for answers when none were available. They all took their art to new heights, stretching traditional methods to meet new challenges. And they all created their own work for themselves, establishing portfolios that showed what they were capable of dreaming and making. None of them waited for that "big break" to find them—they made it for themselves.

We hope that you will find this collective offering as inspiring as we do.

Rafael Jaen, Holly Poe Durbin, and
Christin Essin, Editors

ACKNOWLEDGMENTS

The editors wish to thank the USITT Publications Committee and the early members of the Allied Arts Fields book team, Martha A. Marking and Mike Monsos, whose expertise helped get the preliminary ideas off the ground. We also want to give special thanks to former USITT President and Institute Fellow Mark Shanda, former USITT Vice-President of Communications Michael Mehler, and USITT Executive Director David Grindle for their unwavering support and leadership.

CHAPTER 1

CHERELLE GUYTON

Majestic and Dual Brained

Amber Voner

IMAGE 1.1 *Cherelle Guyton.*
Photo courtesy of Cherelle Guyton.

Feelings of unknowingness began to percolate when contemplating the idea of interviewing a designer in the same field as mine. Early on in my career, to anyone that would listen, I would ask questions around wigs, hair, and makeup; all my senses open, eager to learn more about design and theatre. This time I was not asking questions for guidance, I was asking questions of exploration. I realized I wasn't entering the unknown.

Having a balanced conversation with another wig, hair, and makeup designer gave me a glimpse into her unique experiences with life and art. It allowed a passionate discussion with a fellow creator, expanding my view into the work-world of another. This project created discoveries as well as an opportunity to engage with another creative individual who is navigating through the same career, and she is thriving!

A SPIRIT OF DISCERNMENT

"A free bird is what he called me," Cherelle chuckles, as she affectionately recounts inspiring moments with her grandfather while growing up in the South. Free-spirited, multifaceted, and gracious, coupled with a spirit of discernment and a side of sweet tea, Cherelle has a gift of developing genuine relationships with people from all walks of life.

A native of Columbia, South Carolina, Cherelle Guyton's road to becoming a professional encompasses years of grit (yes, cheese grits as well), self-awareness, a steady grind, intense practice, and passion accompanied by quick wit and a peculiar sense of humor.

IMAGE 1.2 *Guyton's in-process for the Oregon Shakespeare Festival.*
Photo courtesy of Cherelle Guyton.

IMAGE 1.3 *Guyton's wig design for* Destiny of Desire *(2018): Vilma Silva.*
Photo by Jenny Graham.[1]

Ms. Guyton is an alumna of the University of South Carolina where she earned her BA in Theatre with a concentration in Costume, Wig, and Makeup Design. A few years after graduation she started her own business, C Stylez U, LLC. Intertwining business with design meant forty hours a week at the bank, running her theatrical wig and makeup design company, attending grad school in the evenings and weekends, helping with her baby niece, and picking up local stagehand work with Broadway in Columbia. During this time, she also served on the University of South Carolina's Black Alumni Council Board, holding positions as Secretary (2012–2013) and President (2013–2014). Her impeccable work ethic and constant grind afforded her an MBA from Webster University along with an MFA certification in Period Hair and Wig Design from the University of South Carolina.

Keeping a focus on the financial aspects at the forefront of her vision propelled Cherelle in expanding her dreams: "Working in banking allowed me to learn about people and processes, what I did not want to become, and how I did not want to be stuck in a rut of basing my life decisions on societal norms and others opinions in regards to my career." The light of Cherelle Guyton's vision is to "not only provide, but to strive and to thrive in business."

IMAGE 1.4 *Guyton's hair/wig design for the Oregon Shakespeare Festival's* Romeo and Juliet *(2018): Christiana Clark.* Photo by Jenny Graham.[2]

MAKING A LIVING OUT OF PURSUING HER DREAM

"I've been blessed to have very supportive parents, family, friends, teachers, and wise counsel," Guyton says. Her artistic expression was supported early in life through adulthood significantly by her mother, who supported Cherelle's participation in various recreational activities along with the drama club at school, church, and in all of her year-round enrichment programs. Extracurricular activities included art, chemistry, dance (all types), engineering and computer science, French, swimming, theatre, and even wrestling. These experiences instilled in her a commitment to being smarter, working three to four times harder, and having a strong work ethic. Family instilled history and culture in her as well. "I still remember my mother hauling me all over town to rehearsals and practices," she says. "My mother went without pursuing some of her own dreams so that we could pursue our dreams. She has always supported my dreams . . . I can never repay her for all of the sacrifices she has made; but I'm going to try."

Coming from a family of brilliant minds, Cherelle's mother was the major motivator as she encouraged her to expand her horizons from an individual freelancer to an official business. C Stylez U, LLC was founded in Columbia, South Carolina, in August 2009, as a means to manifest her dreams of being a theatrical hair/wig and makeup designer while pursuing her entrepreneurial goals. As we speak, Cherelle's passion is apparent, along with her left-brained entrepreneurial visions. "I like to create art but I like money, too," she states as she bursts into a boisterous fit of laughter. This philosophy of balance has guided her entrepreneurial journey, allowing her to establish a successful, bicoastal creative business, specializing in hair/wig and makeup design services for theatre, TV/film, photography, marketing, and private clientele. Ms. Guyton has designed over thirty-five productions to date, with this year being a pinnacle in her career as the first hair and wig designer in the Oregon Shakespeare Festival's (OSF) eighty-three years of existence. While living her dream career at OSF, she uses both sides of her brain in her role as head of the wig and hair department and the salon director.

COMMUNICATION AND ATMOSPHERE

Cherelle Guyton has an empathic approach to team building, creating balance while optimizing all of the talents presented. "Take the pulse, find out what people want to do and what they are interested in, and honor that as much as you can," she says. As the head of the wig and hair department at OSF she feels strongly about inclusion. Ms. Guyton has experienced many different types of work situations, each contributing to her clear understanding of teamwork: "My team can't help me and

IMAGE 1.5 *Guyton with her team.*
Photo courtesy of Cherelle Guyton.

I can't help my team if there's no open communication."

Respectful communication allows communal delegation and reverence around the creative process: "Process, it's all about the process—to remain collaborative we've got to keep it in black and white, so that we can all see it, so that we can all keep up with it and delegate what needs to be done to whomever is most interested and able to do it, then we create a plan." A collaborative map is hung in Cherelle's work rooms for the team to remain abreast of the actively changing and shifting schedules of the repertory.

BALANCE

In discussing running her own business, operating a full-time position at OSF, and attending to her familial obligations, the topic of balance was sparked. Keeping a well-organized space, properly preparing and planning, committing only to inspiring work, and frugally guarding her time are practices that Cherelle abides by for a healthy work–life balance. "To produce at the level I want to produce at I am unable to give my time freely to unproductive situations, individuals or foolishness where there is not going to be a positive outcome or any productivity for myself, the company and/or the community."

As an innovative and versatile designer, educator, artist, and entrepreneur with more than fifteen years of experience in theatre, Guyton balances her multiple obligations through a process of compartmentalization and prioritization. According to Guyton, "It's a lifestyle." Cherelle is a unique individual with no interest in diluting herself for a fear-based mentality that society uses to oppress minorities. By staying logical, analytical, and mission focused, together with thoughtfulness and strong intuition, Cherelle has mastered the ability to use both sides of her brain, successfully connecting a world of fantasy with her own real-life fairy tale.

Ms. Guyton operates with clarity of who she is and what type of work she seeks to produce. When shifts in the capacity of a commitment emerge or when urgencies impose on the creative process, Cherelle does not deter from working to her full capacity. "If there is a drastic shift in the design from what we discussed or we've previously discussed the need for resources and they aren't in place, we need to go back to the table." A respectful, open, and explorative conversation about the continuation of the creative process will occur when needed.

Before life is breathed into the hair and wig designs on stage, Cherelle's personal relationship with the work is conceived. "I am unable to put my name on work that as a whole, as a unit, doesn't fully represent who I am and what my values and missions are."

DESIGN TRACK/WOMAN OF COLOR

"I love transforming people, telling their story through their hair and makeup." As a young, black millennial she is paving the way for future artists, generously sharing her knowledge through teaching and designing from the heart. A holistic approach is her guiding principle, enabling an overall cohesive design aesthetic. A scribble on a piece of paper here, a color swatch of hair weft there, all explorations that at one point in time only belonged to Cherelle, heavily influence her designs and work.

IMAGE 1.6 *Guyton working on a wig for the Oregon Shakespeare Festival in her well-organized workspace.*
Photo by Julie Cortez.

IMAGE 1.7 *Guyton's finished wigs for the Oregon Shakespeare Festival's* Romeo and Juliet *(2018): Ensemble. Clockwise starting with the bloodied person on the floor: Sara Bruner, Armando McClain, Kyle Sanderson, Ethan Hennes, Richard Elmore, and Monique Holt.*
Photo by Jenny Graham.[3]

Conversations get deeper as thoughts around privilege within the industry arise, with Guyton noting, "I have had to carve out my own track in regards to pursuing hair makeup and wig design."

Guyton is at the forefront at breaking societal standards, creating space for inclusion in theatre. "Design is about people! Consideration of the actor being in a mandatory hairstyle that hundreds to thousands of people will see them in, multiple times per week over the course of weeks, months and possibly years."

Guyton connects through conversation and paying attention to social cues. "Look at a person and find out who they are, understand that they are living breathing organisms that have brains, comprehension and process levels, they have read the script and know their character."

IMAGE 1.8 *Guyton's finished wigs for Disney's* Beauty and the Beast *(2017): Jordan Barbour, Jennie Greenberry.*
Photo by Jenny Graham.[4]

Keeping the authenticity of the person and translating it into their character, designs are inspired and infused with connection and understanding. Guyton shows real care about natural hair, creating a personal look, and making a customized experience for the performer.

This self-proclaimed Southern belle is leading the nation as a pioneer of diverse, authentic, and inclusive hair and wig designs in American theatre. She uses a humanistic approach, constantly collecting ideas to feed her creative drive while taking a genuine deep dive into the individual performers assuming the role. As an expert in the field of theatrical wig, hair, and makeup design, her process involves creating hair, wig, and makeup designs that dually represent the performers' ethnicities while maintaining the design integrity of the characters they are portraying.

INFLUENCES AND TECHNIQUES

Guyton is grateful to her early influences. She says, "Valerie Pruett and Lisa Martin Stuart were two of my most influential professors at the University of South Carolina. They loved and cared for me as an individual while simultaneously understanding challenges that I faced as a person of color—without being condescending, overbearing or just plain fake. They are genuine women who pushed and protected me when needed. They invested time, energy and teaching in me. I will forever be grateful to Ms. Valerie and Ms. Lisa, my professors at Carolina."

She also mentions how an article entitled "Dream Weaver" sent by a friend many years ago influenced her. "It was about Adele Thorpe, an African-American hair weaver and wig designer. This woman was designing hair and wigs for theatre, television, film, and recording artists in New York in 2004. My friend said, 'If she can do it, you can do it.'" She still has the article—it's on her vision board. This woman, without even knowing it, has been a source of inspiration and motivation for Cherelle Guyton.

FINAL THOUGHTS

I was inspired by my conversations with Cherelle revolving around saying "yes" to work that fully represents who you are, and the values and missions that you believe in. Is it really a luxury to feel a connection to the projects that you choose to do? Maybe it's more of a necessity, or perhaps it's a form of self-care. These points reminded me that it is necessary to do work that feeds me and to design shows that resonate with me as a human being and as a designer. I want to explore these ideas further, digging deeper into the idea of only saying "yes" to projects where I feel a connection.

Knowing when to say "no" takes time, experience, and a whole lot of self-understanding. Guyton has mastered this with grace and has reminded me of the importance of the intent of a project. Design, like life, is not a linear process, but rather a spiral of content, collaboration, and constant evaluation. Standing tall and proud behind the message and content of a project cannot just be a luxury; it is truthful design, it is inner design, it is the ability to self-express. Ideas and experiences mixed with research and discovery work in synergy, forming an understanding and then creative freedom.

Our name and legacy are connected to the art we create, existing long after a show has come and gone. Choosing projects that we believe in allows the creation of a symbiotic relationship between the design and the designer. My "yes" means more when I can say "no." This project allowed me discoveries that have expanded my view. When a project makes my soul sing and creates questions about my human existence, here is where I thrive; it's where I want to be and what I hope for all theatre artists.

ARTIST BIO

While leading with authenticity in creating characters' hair and wig design, Cherelle Guyton is an innovative and versatile designer, educator, artist, and entrepreneur with more than fifteen years of experience in theatre. Currently, Cherelle is the hair/wig supervisor and salon director at the Oregon Shakespeare Festival (OSF). Cherelle is returning to OSF for her fifth season, and is ecstatic as she has the opportunity to design one of her all-time favorite Shakespeare works, *Romeo and Juliet*. Cherelle is the first hair/wig designer in the OSF's eighty-three years of existence.

While living her dream career at OSF, she continues to operate her bicoastal costume, wig, and makeup design business, C Stylez U, LLC. C Stylez U currently offers a variety of costume, wig, and makeup design services for theatre, TV/film, photography, marketing, and private clientele. Her repertoire includes Broadway on Tour and onstage/backstage experience in theatre, film, and television.

Cherelle enjoys engaging in her current and native communities through design, educational workshops, and seminars. Cherelle's career goals include being a multifaceted designer in an array of industries while strengthening awareness, furthering knowledge, and enhancing costume, hair, wig, and makeup design aesthetics through an authentic, equitable, diverse, and inclusive lens.

IMAGE 1.9 *Guyton at her office.*
Photo courtesy of Cherelle Guyton.

NOTES

1. Production: *Destiny of Desire* by Karen Zacarías, Oregon Shakespeare Festival, 2018. Director: José Luis Valenzuela. Music: Rosino Serrano. Scenic design: Francois Pierre Couture. Costume design: Julie Weiss. Lighting design: Pablo Santiago. Sound design: John Zalewski. Dramaturg: Julie Felise Dubiner. Voice and text director: Robert Ramirez. Music director: Deborah Wicks La Puma. Choreographer: Robert Barry Fleming. Assistant costume design: Carolyn Mazuca. Fight director: U. Jonathan Toppo.
2. Production: *Romeo and Juliet* by William Shakespeare, Oregon Shakespeare Festival, 2018. Director: Dámaso Rodríguez. Scenic design: Efren Delgadillo, Jr. Costume design: Leah Piehl. Hair and wig design: Cherelle Guyton. Lighting design: Tom Ontiveros. Composer/sound design: Rodolfo Ortega. Dramaturg: Tiffany Ana López. Voice and text director: Rebecca Clark Carey. Sign coach/VGC interpreter: Kalen Feeney. Movement and intimacy director: Sarah Lozoff. Fight director: U. Jonathan Toppo.

Production stage manager: D. Christian Bolender.

3. See note 3.
4. Production: *Beauty and the Beast*, Oregon Shakespeare Festival, 2017. Music: Alan Menken. Lyrics: Howard Ashman and Tim Rice. Book: Linda Woolverton. Director: Eric Tucker. Cast: Daniel T. Parker, Robin Goodrin Nordli, Britney Simpson, David Kelly, and Kate Mulligan. Costume designer: Ana Kuzmanic.

CHAPTER 2

ANYTHING BUT A STRAIGHT LINE!

Peter S. Miller, Scenic Artist

Anthony R. Phelps

IMAGE 2.1 *Peter S. Miller.*
Photo courtesy of Peter Miller.

"You don't know at the beginning where you will end up in your career." Peter Miller says this to theatre artists just starting out. Miller is a scenic artist in New York City whose career has encompassed film, television, Broadway, and opera. He has also been the paint charge at the Juilliard School. He is a rich resource on the subjects of trompe l'oeil painting, historical backdrop painting, Styrofoam carving, molding and casting, and aging and distressing scenery. Few know that his career path to becoming a scenic artist has been anything but a straight line, and his words to early career artists come from experience.

COLLABORATION AND STORYTELLING

Ask Peter Miller what a scenic artist does and you won't get the answer you expect. You might expect him to say that a scenic artist paints scenery, hangs wallpaper, and plasters walls. His answer is based less in techniques and tasks and more in the collaboration and storytelling he feels a scenic artist does. To him, a scenic artist's job is to "interpret and magnify the scenic designer and director's vision of the work." The scenic designer may create the scenic world of the play, but the scenic artist supplies additional information to the story that isn't obvious in the text.

IMAGE 2.2 *Fire escape tower units for* A Bronx Tale*. Design by Beowulf Boritt. Painted at Showman Fabricators with Nancy Orr and Everett O'Neil.*
Photo courtesy of Peter Miller.

IMAGE 2.3 *Detail of flaking paint texture.*
Photo courtesy of Peter Miller.

The scenic artist asks new questions, fleshing out detail not found in the broader stokes of the scenic designer's vision. Does an interior apartment set look new and freshly painted, or does it look dingy and used? Are there handprints around the doorknobs and light switches indicating heavy usage? Does the paint on the molding appear thick and sloppily slathered on, possibly by a building superintendent who is rushing the job?

"When working with a scenic designer in theatre or opera if you can get them to give you three sentences about the concept it is very helpful in making decisions in interpreting the designer's work," Miller says.

When describing his work in film and television, Miller says, "most of our work involves enhancing existing locations to reinforce a story point or hiding things (like air conditioners or exit signs) that are wrong for the story the scenery needs to tell. When we paint a set that is built in the studio, most of the time it has to look as 'real' as possible; the viewer should think that the set is an actual place."

FROM LEWIS TO ZEFFIRELLI

Growing up in Johnson, Vermont, Miller began a lifelong interest in Medieval and Renaissance history through *The Chronicles of Narnia* books by C. S. Lewis. This led to his mother taking him to see Franco Zeffirelli's film version of Shakespeare's *Romeo and Juliet* when he was in the third grade. The 1968 film won Academy Awards for Best Cinematography and Best Costume Design, and it was also nominated for Best Director and Best Picture. The visually stunning film was financially successful, and was the last Shakespearean film to be nominated for Best Picture. Upon seeing the film, Miller wanted to become a Shakespearean actor. Seeking any exposure to Shakespeare he could, Miller would spend hours listening to recordings of Shakespeare's plays. Hearing the text spoken out loud by great actors rather than reading it in a book was crucial. Miller went to the Champlain Shakespeare Festival in Burlington, Vermont, when he was ten years old. This eventually led to an apprenticeship at the Champlain Shakespeare Festival in the summers of 1976 and 1977. Miller found that he was interested not only in the acting of the plays, but also the costumes, particularly the armor and other costume crafts. In the pages of *Designing and Making Stage Costumes* by Motley, a young Miller found information about costume crafts that opened doors for him. Through the book, he learned how to make costume props like the crowns, armor, and chain mail that he was imagining. After receiving a copy of the Richard Corson's *Stage Makeup*, he delved into makeup and prosthetics. He became particularly interested in old age and special effects makeup.

SHAKESPEARE'S OLD MEN

With his love of Shakespeare and his newfound passion for costume crafts and makeup, Miller created his own one-man show—*Shakespeare's Kings*—and toured it at the age of fifteen. The show featured five characters from Shakespeare's plays: Polonius, Lear, Prospero, Macbeth, and Titus Andronicus. His show not only demonstrated his skill with the Shakespearean language and his creativity with the makeup and costumes, but also featured a unique special effect. While playing Andronicus, through some theatrical sleight of hand, Miller cut off his hand and brandished a bloody stump. George Dullea from the *New York Times* wrote an article about Miller's one-man show on May 21, 1975, titled "High School Freshman to Shakespearean Heavy." The article went into great detail about Miller's prosthetics, makeup effects, and costume pieces, as well as his performance. A few days after the article came out, Miller received a letter from Dick Smith, known as the godfather of makeup effects. Smith was a part of the early days of television at NBC and had worked on major Academy Award–winning films such as *The Godfather* and *The Godfather Part II*, and later *The Deer Hunter* and *Amadeus*. Smith was well-known to Miller in 1973, having just created Linda Blair's animatronic, 360-degree spinning, pea soup–projectile vomiting, demonized head in *The Exorcist*, an obsession for young fans of movie magic. Smith wrote Miller that he admired his work and if he ever needed any help to reach out and Smith would help if he could. Meanwhile, the *New York Times* article got Miller an invitation to go to New York and appear on the television show *To Tell the Truth* as an old man.

While in New York City, Miller met Dick Smith in person and joined him for the test-fitting of a costume and false-arm effect for Martin Scorsese's Best Picture–nominated film *Taxi Driver*, starring Robert De Niro, which Smith was working on. Smith introduced Miller to the legendary Broadway and film wig maker

IMAGE 2.4 *Costume and makeup for Richard the II, part of Miller's 1976 one-man show,* Shakespeare's Kings.
Photo courtesy of Peter Miller.

and makeup artist Bob Kelly. Over the years Smith was very generous with his time and knowledge with Miller. "Dick Smith is the real reason I started teaching scene painting—it was the only thing I could do to pay him back for his incredible generosity," Miller says. "I was so fortunate that he reached out to me when I was a teenager growing up in a place where nobody had a job creating magic."

THE COLLEGE EXPERIENCE

Miller spent the next few years in Vermont apprenticing at the Champlain Shakespeare Festival and taking classes at Johnson Stage College instead of his high school. He was exposed to more professional theatre as the Ensemble Studio Theatre had a summer residency at Johnson State College in Miller's hometown. Founded in 1968, the Ensemble Studio Theatre produces original and challenging plays to their audiences in New York City.

Miller became friends with actors John Randolph and Sarah Cunningham, who had long careers on the stage and screen. These actors reinforced the idea to Miller and his parents that this was a job people could do, echoing what Dick Smith had told him earlier. An alumnus of Harvard University also saw the *New York Times* article about Miller and reached out to him. He encouraged Miller to apply to Harvard.

Miller applied to Harvard and was accepted and started in the fall of 1978. He became involved in theatre right away, working on a production of Wagner's Ring cycle that was directed by Harvard student and future opera and theatre director Peter Sellers. The production was staged almost entirely with puppets, some of which were created and operated by Miller. While at Harvard, Miller majored in the Visual and Environmental Studies Department, which had a film studies major. The broad overview of the arts would serve him well in his career.

One of the most important courses he took was Fine Arts 13, an art survey course that appealed to his love of history and visual art. As time went on at Harvard, Miller found himself acting less in shows and spending more time creating props and makeup. Miller worked on many productions for the Harvard/Radcliffe Gilbert and Sullivan Players.

IMAGE 2.5 *Act II setting for Gilbert and Sullivan's* Ruddigore. *Set design and painting by Miller for the Harvard/Radcliffe Gilbert and Sullivan Players, 1983.*
Photo courtesy of Peter Miller.

Their "period" production style allowed Miller to use his historical research skills as well as his skills as an artisan. Receiving a copy of the Lynn Pecktal's *Designing and Painting for Theatre*, Miller became inspired to paint more scenery. The book was necessary, because there wasn't anyone to teach him how to paint scenery at Harvard. By the time Miller graduated from Harvard he had not only painted many student productions but had also worked on the paint crew of an early production at American Repertory Theatre that came to Harvard in 1980.

JUILLIARD AND LESTER POLAKOV'S STUDIO

Upon graduation Miller wanted to continue in scenic art rather than makeup and prosthetics. At the time he graduated from Harvard in 1984, slasher movies like *A Nightmare on Elm Street* and *Friday the 13th* were popular at the box office and were a good entry point for people wanting to go into makeup. The characters of Freddy Krueger from *A Nightmare on Elm Street* and Jason from *Friday the 13th* were gory characters. The Krueger character used lots of skin prosthetics to give him the look of having been burnt on his body, including his face and neck. The Jason Voorhees character from *Friday the 13th* was meant to look deformed under his now-iconic hockey mask. Miller decided he wanted to work as a scenic artist in theatre and opera more than working on slasher movies doing lots of blood effects. He also realized he needed more training, as

IMAGE 2.6 *Cartouche on marble background. An example of trompe l'oeil technique.*
Photo courtesy of Peter Miller.

Harvard didn't have a theatre program and he was mostly self-taught. Miller applied to the Juilliard School's Professional Intern Program in Scene Painting, now called the Professional Apprentice Program in Scene Painting. Upon being rejected for the program, he found a job as the designer and technical director at Russell Sage College in Troy, New York. At the same time, he worked as a scenic artist at the Empire State Institute for the Performing Arts in Albany. While working in Albany, he learned about Lester Polakov's studio, New York Studio and Forum of Stage Design, and about United Scenic Artists 829, the union for theatrical designers and scenic artists.

Miller applied again for the Juilliard School program, and this time was accepted, so he moved to New York City. Miller decided to study at Lester Polakov's studio, New York Studio and Forum of Stage Design, on the weekends. Polakov's studio was established in 1958, and Polakov brought in the best scenic, lighting, and costume designers and scenic artists to teach at the studio. Polakov himself was a Broadway designer. His credits, among many, include *Call Me Mister*, *The Member of the Wedding*, *Skin of Our Teeth*, and *Charlotte*. Miller found the approach to scene painting at Juilliard was about thin paints, a watercolor technique with lots of layers and glazes. Polakov's approach was different; the paint was more opaque and there was a greater emphasis on the light source and trompe l'oeil. Miller had a revelation one week where he was painting a faux marble sample at both Juilliard and Polakov's studio. He was able to achieve the same result with two different processes and learned there is always more than one way to achieve an effect.

YOU DON'T KNOW WHERE YOU WILL END UP IN YOUR CAREER

After he finished the program at the Juilliard School and his studies with Lester Polakov, Miller became the paint charge at Juilliard during the academic year and at Wolf Trap Opera in Virginia during the summer. During his time working at Juilliard, Miller found it useful to mingle with the other departments and became a better collaborator. "You don't know where you will end up in your career," Millers says, "and it makes you a better collaborator if you know what other people do and know their vocabulary." While some scenic artists only paint scenery, Miller was able to use his past experiences in costume crafts and props to get projects that straddle the disciplines of paint, sculpture, and collage. For example, his molding and casting experience from makeup effects helped him create a mass grave for a production at Wolf Trap Opera. He often uses materials in unexpected ways, such as creating gigantic candles with wax drips made from silk, PVC pipe, caulk, and Sculpt or Coat for the Broadway musical *Dance of the Vampires*.

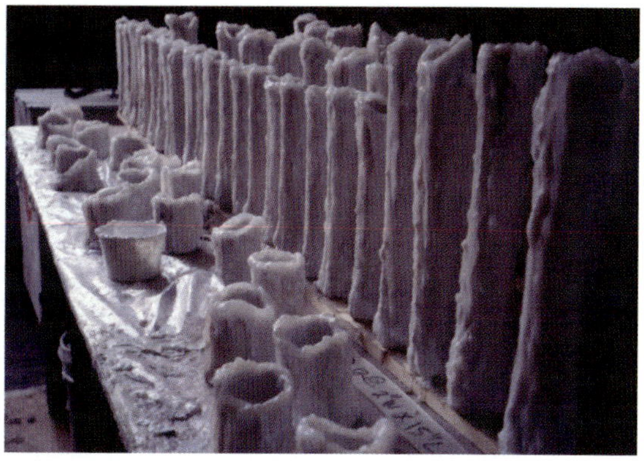

IMAGE 2.7 *Candles created for Broadway's* Dance of the Vampires. *Design by David Gallo, painted with Nancy Orr.*
Photo courtesy of Peter Miller.

SCENIC ARTISTS 829

Miller worked for several seasons as the paint charge at Juilliard before joining United Scenic Artists 829 (USA829) in the category of scenic art. USA829 is the union that represents designers in theatre, opera, and dance and scenic artists in film and television in the Northeast. Miller joined USA829 through the Track A interview and portfolio review. Scenic artists with less experience can take a practical exam. At the exam the scenic artist is presented with a painter's elevation of a small backdrop to produce within an eight-hour time frame. Being a scenic artist in the union enables Miller to work in union shops in New York that produce scenery for Broadway, ballet, and national tours. With his union membership, he can also work on films or television in New York.

Working as a union scenic artist is not the same as working at a full-time staff position. According to Miller, "We are 'per diem employees' hired by the day for a project, but we do receive full benefits for that day." There can be intense periods of work with long hours and lots of overtime, but there can be long periods of unemployment, too. Not everybody can handle the uncertainty of the schedule. Miller finds being in the union has some big advantages over nonunion work. While enabling him to work on Broadway and in film and television, the union also provides negotiating power for wages, safer working conditions, and has health insurance and retirement plans for its vested members.

Miller has now been working as a union scenic artist for twenty-five years. One of his favorite theatre productions was the Tom Stoppard trilogy *The Coast of Utopia* for the Lincoln Center. Miller thought the shows were really good and was impressed that a nine-hour theatre production focusing on philosophical debates in prerevolutionary Russia could be commercially successful. Critics also found *The Coast of Utopia* to be a successful production, nominating it for ten Tony Awards, of which it won seven, including Best Play. As a scenic artist for the production he helped to create

IMAGE 2.8 *Mass grave created for Wolf Trap Opera Company's production of* The Rakes Progress.
Photo courtesy of Peter Miller.

IMAGE 2.9 *Russian serfs created for* The Coast of Utopia. *Design by Scott Pask and Bob Crowly. Created with Nancy Orr, Everett O'Neil, and Cheryl Stewart.*
Photo courtesy of Peter Miller.

the souls of eighty-four Russian serfs out of translucent, plastic Armani mannequins, bubble-wrap, clear packing tape, and a layer of thin, ragged fabric. A December 30, 2006, *New York Times* article by Ginia Bellafante described them as headless and legless with a grim costume of servitude.

Miller worked on two different Broadway productions of *Waiting for Godot*. One production was cast with Sir Ian McKellen and Sir Patrick Stewart, the other with John Goodman and Nathan Lane. He described both as good productions, but markedly different. "One was set in an abandoned, bombed-out Image theatre, the other in a deserted stone quarry," the scenery for each was very textural and dimensional with "lots of foam carving."

IMAGE 2.10 *Santo Loquasto's design for a Broadway production of* Waiting for Godot *set in an abandoned rock quarry on the setup deck at Showman Fabricators with Nancy Orr, Bill Reilly, and Everett O'Neil.*
Photo courtesy of Peter Miller.

FILM CREDITS AND ALLIED FIELDS

Miller's favorite film credit is *Unfaithful*, his second major movie project. He says it was a good script, and there are some excellent performances, especially by Diane Lane, who received an Oscar nomination. He was on the job for most of the project and got to see how a film is made from the beginning until the final "wrap." In addition to film and stage work, Miller has painted displays for Mattel Toys and the Metropolitan Museum of Art.

Projects include the McQueen exhibition *Dangerous Beauty* for the Fashion Institute, the restoration of the carved-foam landscape surrounding the Met's seasonal "Angel Tree," and Cornelia Parker's roof garden installation *Transitional Object* (PsychoBarn).

A point Miller makes is that sometimes you create really cool things for sometimes not very good projects and other times you might do boring things for a really great finished project. "It might be more fun to create alien rocks for a sci-fi action film that might not be very good than painting flats institutional green for an Academy Award–winning film." He adds, "I try to remind myself that I am getting paid to create magic every day and many people would like to have my job. I like making fake things that appear real."

In his more than thirty years in show business Miller has seen a number of changes in working conditions and technology. He says that thanks to the work of industrial hygienist Monona Rossol, who works as the

Health and Safety Director for USA829 and the International Alliance of Theatrical Stage Employees (IATSE), movie sets and scene shops have become much safer. He says there is much more awareness of safety precautions for the use of sprays and different types of foam products. Locations of movie sets and scene shops are much safer with regards to exposure to lead or asbestos and the proper disposal of paints and solvents.

Over his career many new products have come on the market for painters, and other products, such as aniline dye, have left the market. He doesn't feel that the basics of painting have changed that much due to technology, but notes that the new high-definition cameras and televisions have changed the necessary finish quality of the paint treatments, particularly in television. In older television sets you often could not see small imperfections in the scenery like screw heads or seams between flats, but the new televisions show all those details. Green screens have taken away some work from scenic artists in film. Movie backings or backdrops seen in the distance through the windows or open doorways used to be painted by hand or were enlarged photographs known as "translights." Now many have been replaced by green screens, which are used to add computer-generated imagery (CGI) later during postproduction. Green screens can also be used to extend the height of the scenery so all of it doesn't need to be built anymore, according to Miller. You can create the bottom level of the set that the actors will interact with and extend the height of it with the green screen so it can look like a really tall room or building in wide camera shots.

On Broadway, many of the multilocation shows are using unit sets instead of the more traditional series of backdrops and scenic units. A lot more sophisticated projection work is being done on Broadway as well. Some of the projection work has eliminated the need for some painted scenery.

Miller also sees how 3D printing and the CNC router have taken over some of the work that scenic artists used to do. These new technologies now do some of the repetitive work that scenic artists used to do in foam carving or molding and casting. Miller has no worry that his job will be taken over anytime soon by a new technology. The pieces created by these new machines still need to be finished by a scenic artist.

PETER MILLER'S FORMULA

Miller works consistently, but still maintains a portfolio and keeps it up-to-date. He uses a paper flipbook-type of portfolio, which is easy to take on the subway and show in an office or on a shop table. He has lots of process shots of his work. Miller does find it hard to photograph much of his film and television work due to nondisclosure agreements that scenic artists sign at the beginning of such projects.

Miller thinks this a rewarding career, but has some words of advice for those interested in the field. As stated earlier, "You don't know at the beginning where you will end up in your career." Miller believes that most people will end up doing something different than they start out thinking they are going to do. The best way to prepare for this is to learn as much as you can about what everybody else is doing. "Ultimately it will make you a better collaborator, and if you have to change jobs at some point in the course of your career, you will have a better understanding of the other possibilities available to you." A broad knowledge base also makes it easier to troubleshoot potential problems. For example, as a scenic artist it is good to know what actors are wearing on their feet when deciding how to texture a rough wood floor. Learning about the other roles also shows respect for what other people do and allows one to continue learning their craft.

Even with his training at Juilliard, Harvard, and with Lester Polakov, Miller still wishes he had a better fine arts background, similar to that of some other scenic artists. Specifically, he wishes he had more formal training in drawing and illustration, as it would be helpful when he has to paint portraits or figurative work. He also thinks that many are unrealistic about how much paying theatre work there is available to recent college graduates as opposed to other aspects of the entertainment industry.

In the academic world, they say "theatre," but what we really should be saying is "show business." According to Miller, "It's hard to make a living doing theatre exclusively." He advises that students should seek out work in film, television, industrials, and all parts of the entertainment field if they want to be regularly employed. Once a person starts working, it can be hard to decide which jobs to take. "When you are in college or even in high school, you understand that this is your passion; that this is where you belong, that these people are your tribe, and that you want to create magic and get paid to do it. Finding out where your talent lies, developing the skills, getting other people to recognize it, and then making a living at it is a much longer journey—there are many paths you can take and some detours along the way. Finding a balance between art, commerce, and simple survival, especially in a competitive environment like New York City is always tricky. Miller has a rubric that he uses to help him quantify the variables and decide if he should take on a project".

MILLER'S RUBRIC

Miller has four questions he asks himself and that other artists can incorporate into their decision-making:

1. ***Is it artistically rewarding?*** Is this a project you always wanted to do? Do you like this playwright? Is it a good script, or do you like the production concept?
2. ***How does this project advance my career?*** Will I get to work with different people? Or with a new technology? Am I working in a different region of the country? Will it get good press?
3. ***Who do I get to work with?*** Are these people I know? Are they my friends? Are they good at their jobs? Are they pleasant and collaborative? Are they new people whom I can make contact with and broaden my network? Will it be fun?
4. ***How much does it pay?*** Find out how much it pays, but also be clear about what is being asked of you. If you are you being hired to be the paint charge, how big is your crew? Or are you a crew of one? Are you expected to paint the props as well? Is it a long- or short-term commitment? Is it a flat rate or are you paid by the hour? If you are paid by the hour, is there overtime? Is food or housing included?

Miller says that you will almost never have a project that satisfies all four of these questions;

IMAGE 2.11 *Gaston's Tavern translucent backdrop for Disney's* Beauty and the Beast, *road company. Variety Scenic Studios with Jane Snow, Nancy Orr, and Alan Trumpler.*
Photo courtesy of Peter Miller.

IMAGE 2.12 *Egyptian temple drop from Hasty Pudding Theatricals'* The Jewel of Denial. *Example of exaggerated, forced perspective. Design by Miller, painting by Cobalt Studios.*
Photo courtesy of Peter Miller.

it might happen once or twice in a lifetime. Some degree of compromise is almost always needed. You might find a project working with great people on a fun show, but the pay isn't great. Or you might have a show that pays well but it won't advance your career and it isn't artistically satisfying. If you can find a project that satisfies three of the four questions, you should seriously consider taking it. If it satisfies two of the questions you should consider the project but be cautious. If the project only satisfies one of these questions, you should turn it down—unless you haven't worked for a long time and you really need the money!

While working full time as a scenic artist Miller has found ways to mentor young scenic artists over the years, and to lend his knowledge to others as Dick Smith had done for him years ago. He taught a scene painting course at the Mason Gross School of the Arts at Rutgers University for six years on weekends. Miller teaches in the USA829 Scenic Artist Apprentice and Training Program. The three-year program offers classes and training for apprentices and assigns them work in scene shops and various film and TV productions in New York City.

He has been a panelist on several discussions at the annual United States Institute for Theatre Technology conference. Every fall, Miller returns to Harvard University to teach in the First-Year Arts Program, a pre-freshman weeklong introduction to the arts at Harvard that culminates in a short musical pageant complete with lighting, costumes, and a painted backdrop produced by the students that Miller teaches.

Since 1989, Miller has been the resident scenic designer for the annual Hasty Pudding Show at Harvard, which often features several turn-of-the-century–style backdrops he designs. Miller has shared his knowledge by writing fifteen articles for the publication *The Painter's Journal* and has served as a theatre history advisor for Curtains Without Borders, a preservation/restoration group in New England that preserves nineteenth-century and early twentieth-century painted backdrops and grand drapes often found in old town halls. Miller expects to be busy in the years to come, and finds there is always more to be learned about one's craft. After thirty years in show business, he can honestly say that he has hardly ever been bored and that he has almost always been amused.

ARTIST BIO

Peter S. Miller grew up in a small Vermont town, where a childhood obsession with Shakespeare led to scene painting. After graduation from Harvard, he moved to New York City to study the craft with Lester Polakov while interning at the Juilliard School. After several seasons as the charge artist at Juilliard and the Wolf Trap Opera Company, he joined Local 829 of United Scenic Artists. He has worked on the paint crews of various stage, film, display, and television productions. Broadway highlights include *Beauty and the Beast, The Little Mermaid, The 25th Annual Putnam County Spelling Bee, A Bronx Tale, The Seagull, Saint Joan, Seascape, The Diary of Anne Frank, Twelfth Night, King Lear*, two revivals of *Waiting for Godot*, and Tom Stoppard's epic trilogy *The Coast of Utopia* for Lincoln Center. Film credits include *War of the Worlds, The Dark Tower,*

Teenage Mutant Ninja Turtles I and *II*, *The Dictator*, *The Stepford Wives*, *The Interpreter*, *Revolutionary Road*, *Doubt*, *It's Complicated*, and *Unfaithful*. Television, display, and streaming credits include Food Network, the World Wrestling Federation's *Grand Slam Highway to Hell*, *The Good Wife*, and seasons 1 and 2 of the *Marvelous Mrs. Maisel* for Amazon Prime. He has also worked on the live NBC productions of *The Sound of Music*, *The Wiz*, and *Jesus Christ Superstar*. Miller has conducted scene painting workshops and sessions at United States Institute for Theatre Technology. He has also taught at Rutgers University and designed for Harvard's The Hasty Pudding Theatricals. He teaches scene painting for Harvard's First-Year Arts Program and the USA829 Apprenticeship and Training Program.

CHAPTER 3

JUDY ADAMSON, COSTUME DRAPER AND MENTOR

Ashley Bellet

IMAGE 3.1 *Judy Adamson received the USITT 2012 Distinguished Achievement Award in Education.* Photo courtesy of R. Finkelstein.

In costume shops around the United States, drapers and first hands lean into their tables, reaching to measure, cut, and pattern. Designers let their eyes wander over dress forms, measuring lines and proportions, planning details, choosing closures and trims. Stitchers crouch behind sewing machines or beneath voluminous skirts, marking, hemming, and finishing each garment. Every line, every stitch highlights the skill of these artisans. Judy Adamson, draper, mentor, professor, and head of Costume Technology at the University of North Carolina at Chapel Hill, has spent a lifetime not only perfecting these skills, but also passing them on to the next generation of technicians. She built one of the first master's degree programs in Costume Technology in the United States and has worked in major regional theatres across the country. Every costume shop depends on its trained artisans, and it is their combination of skills that breathe three-dimensional life into the ideas of costume designers. Empowering young makers with these skills, training them in the arts of planning and assemblage, are at the heart of Judy Adamson's lifelong career in draping and costume making.

In March of 2018, Adamson and I sat down to talk at a picnic table during a busy day at the national United States Institute for Theatre Technology (USITT) conference in Fort Lauderdale, Florida. We had managed to squeeze in a couple hours between commission meetings and poster sessions, and Adamson left her group of mentees with a colleague so she could tell me about her career in costume making. "Making" is Adamson's term, and she is very clear about the vocabulary she uses to describe her work. The words "build" and "construct" make her grimace: "I don't like the word 'build.' That's something I learned from my mentor, Barbara Matera. She hated the word 'build,' just hated it! If you say, 'Oh I have to go to a fancy dinner!' do you *build* yourself a dress, or *make* yourself a dress? I guess there are some people who say that, but I look at them and say, 'Really?'"

Adamson's emphasis on "making" is not just about the linguistics—it speaks to a much more integral relationship between the maker, the garment, and the artist who wears it. "Why would you treat a costume differently than the clothes you wear? The word 'build' implies something of less value than *making* a specific costume for a specific person. You're creating clothes for an actor to wear onstage. If you don't treat them with a certain amount of respect—if their clothes are well done and they look good on the inside, and they look like real clothes to them, then they treat them that way. The integrity of the costume speaks to the integrity of your relationship with the actors . . . You make clothes, you sew dresses. We're dressmakers."

I thought for a moment about some favorite garments from my own wardrobe. A tweed blazer, a hand-painted dress, a blousy silk tunic—each one is well made, and I take care to follow laundering instructions and hang these pieces much more gently than knit tank tops and inexpensive Oxford shirts captured from sales racks at the mall. The integrity of a garment translates to how the owner cares for it—not just in theatre, but in our daily lives. I smiled while imagining her disgust at fast fashion; makers notice the details, because they live those details. Those details are the ones that provide integrity and longevity, not just for the garment but for the craft itself.

Details like this—the ones not relegated to the shop but to the community and personality of her profession—are central to Adamson's passion for costume making, and have stuck with her throughout her distinguished career. She is concerned with how costume technologists and their colleagues understand the craft, and how this craft fits into the larger picture. Adamson is also deeply invested in how her students view their own contribution to the profession, both as artisans and as technologists with a passion for the details. While her years at Barbara Matera's Costume House in New York City are when she "truly learned the trade," Adamson discovered her love of sewing years before.

Adamson first learned how to sew in 4-H club while in high school in Iowa. At the time she enjoyed being on stage, and found her way to the theatre department when she attended the State College of Iowa, now the University of Northern Iowa. When I asked if she was a good actress, Adamson hesitated in her story: "Well . . . I *acted*. I believe I was playing Marianna in *Measure for Measure* when I said I do NOT want to do this." When her faculty mentor asked if she had any other skills, she replied "I can sew." The rest of her years in college were spent with Monabelle Hake in the costume shop. "I had reinforcement all along. I had a lot of wonderful mentors."

After college she and her husband worked at several theatres—he was on stage, and she worked in the costume shop. While he completed his graduate studies in Chapel Hill, Adamson found a home in the University of North Carolina (UNC) costume shop.

IMAGE 3.2 *Fitting for Ann Hould Ward's dress for the Tony Awards for* Beauty and the Beast. *Barbara Matera fitting room, June 1994. Milka (dressmaker), David Lawrence (hair designer for the show), Ann Hould Ward, Judy Adamson, and Barbara Matera.*

Photo courtesy of Judy Adamson.

"Bobbi Owen—she was new out of school—she had just started there. I worked in the shop for a year, and then I started teaching construction. After my third year, UNC started Playmakers' Repertory. They began to bring in drapers and craftspeople from outside to work on the shows, people like Mindy Sorkin and Polly P. Smith. They were really inspirations to me because I knew that I was capable of doing what they were doing. That was something that I wanted to do."

I asked if she had ever considered a profession in costume design. She responded quickly: "No, never design." From the beginning, Adamson has understood her worth as a costume maker, and when she and her husband left Chapel Hill she pulled together her resume to submit to costume houses around New York City. Adamson knew she could sew, but she herself admits that the interview process was a bit new to her, especially in a new city. During an early interview with Milo Morrow, the head of the costume shop at the New York Shakespeare Festival, he said, "Well this is pretty good, but you're gonna work for Barbara Matera."

Established in 1967, Barbara Matera, Ltd. was a leading New York costume shop known for its attention to intricate details and couture methods; Matera's shop attracted top Broadway designers and constructed thousands of costumes for theatres, operas, ballets, and film studios across the country. In her 2011 article in *Theatre Technology and Design*, draper Triffin Morris describes how Matera came to work in New York City for Ray Diffen—a fellow British costume maker—but soon went out on her own to establish a shop with her husband, Arthur Matera. Throughout her years in the costume business, Barbara Matera was praised for the combination of skill and creativity she brought not only to her work, but also to the work of the designers who relied upon her. As an integral part of the lineage of New York City costume shops, Matera trained many young drapers and dressmakers who would go one to build their own businesses and training programs around the country.

Within days Morrow's prediction for Adamson came true. Sitting across from me with her hands linked together, Adamson smiled at the memory of her interview with Barbara. "I was lucky, and she was so kind to me—she wasn't really interested in my portfolio. She just said, 'You like to sew?' And I said yes. 'Well ok, then,' she said. 'You start on Monday. Fine, just show up, $5.50 an hour.'" And that, according to Adamson, began her real education in

IMAGE 3.3 *Amy VanderStaay, Jennifer McMillan, and Judy Adamson working on* Carmen *for the Carolina Ballet in the workroom at the University of North Carolina at Chapel Hill, 1999.*
Photo courtesy of Judy Adamson.

professional costume making. "I started out just sewing, sitting at a table with the hand finishers, and occasionally they would need people to stay late and do things and I always volunteered."

Over the course of our conversation, Adamson listed every teacher she had and every interested mentor who affected her work, pressing her finger into the table as she named each one—"Tom Schmuck, Monabelle Hake . . ."—each holds a place in her memory and her career. She speaks most fondly of Barbara, however, as the woman who both taught her to sew and inspired her to want to create beautiful things.

Working with a knowledgeable, powerful mentor like Barbara Matera makes a huge difference in a young technician's life, as it did for Adamson. When I asked if she could sum up the most important things she learned in the first year at such a legendary studio, she quickly cut me off: "The first year? More like the first couple of *days*! I'd never seen so many people hand basting and doing hand work. That was incredible! I impressed Barbara all along, I think, because I wasn't afraid of the sewing machine. I could do anything with a sewing machine. My bad sewing was better than most people's good sewing," she said with a wink, and we both chuckled. "I was really confident in my ability. But I quickly learned that those ladies knew far more than I did. And you know, that's where I started to learn from the other dressmakers."

IMAGE 3.4 *Working in Barbara Matera's studio on* Sleeping Beauty *for the New York City Ballet, designed by Patricia Zipprodt, 1991.*
Photo courtesy of Judy Adamson.

She may have started at Matera's hand-sewing table, but Adamson quickly worked her way up to drapers' assistant—"we weren't called first hands, but drapers' assistants"—and finally to draper. The terminology is important: she pointed out that the union—the International Ladies' Garment Workers Union—used the terms "operator" (those who used the machines) and "finisher" (those who completed the hand work). All of the women in the studio called themselves "dressmakers," and this distinction continues to define Adamson's approach to making clothes.

"Barbara was just an amazing draper. I took her drapes apart to make the pattern, true it up—I learned a lot of pattern making skills from her." I have personally had the opportunity to see some incredibly skilled drapers at work, but I can only imagine working with Barbara Matera. Drapers are the primary agents of communication between the designer and the three-dimensional costume—they're the ones who look at a rendering and translate that aesthetic into fabric on the dress form. Drapers must be skilled at patterning and tailoring, using a combination of historical techniques, adaptation, and improvisation. They connect directly with the designer, and they must know what questions to ask and how to ask them in a way that will inform their own processes. Precision is important, but speed and efficiency are as well. Drapers must lead their teams in the shop, passing off their patterns to a first hand, who, in turn, cuts the pattern and fabric

IMAGE 3.5 *Fitting the Chesterfield coat on Asta for* Nick and Nora, *an updated version of* The Thin Man, *designed by Theoni V. Aldredge, 1991. Every member of the cast had a Chesterfield coat as a disguise, even Asta!*
Photo courtesy of Judy Adamson.

accordingly and hands it off to their stitcher. Now, I use the term "hand off" loosely here—the draper also supervises the process. Their job is not just creation; they must also focus on how the garment goes together. Decisions like closures, seam finishes, linings, and hems often fall to the draper and their interpretation of the rendering, especially if the designer is not on site. Thus, the draper must see and care for the details while maintaining the broader vision.

Drapers must also have strong interpersonal communication skills—they are a third of the communication triangle that forms in the fitting room. Designer, performer, draper—these three voices are key in making sure a costume is functional, fitted precisely, and fits into the design. When a designer and draper work together over several shows they can build a common language. Similarly, when a draper works with their first hand and stitchers over a long period of time, they can also find comfortable working practices that make their process more efficient. Of course, when a draper knows their team really well, that kind of history leads to lots of great stories.

When I asked if Barbara was precise in her draping, Adamson smiled and rolled her eyes. "Well, yes. There's a great story about Miss Hannigan's dress. It was for a production of *Annie*, years and years ago. Every time we had to rebuild it or make a new one, we pulled out that same pattern, and the same dressmaker put it together. One time, that dressmaker wasn't there, so it was passed to another person—and we realized how messed up that pattern was!"

When a draper feels comfortable with what they have draped on the dress form, they remove the muslin and begin the process of truing it up. This takes a lot of attention to detail and a fair bit of mathematical precision: seams should be the same length so they match up; centerlines and side seams should be straight to fall smoothly on the body; curves should meet at ninety-degree angles for smooth transitions. Drapers even-out their seam allowances, label each pattern piece, and make sure that all their curves and armscyes match up. This is where precision is most important.

Adamson laughs about how they fussed with the Miss Hannigan pattern. "That dressmaker always just made it work. They had worked together for so many years—she just

IMAGE 3.6 *Judy Adamson at her worktable in the Matera Workroom, 1993.*
Photo courtesy of Judy Adamson.

learned to make it work. It was easier for her to just figure it out on her end. Barbara was incredible, but she had a relationship with her shop that sometimes let her . . . well, she let her staff figure it out for her."

This is the kind of story I love. Barbara Matera's reputation is unquestionable, and her skills are what made her shop a cornerstone for the professional costume world. Her reliance on her staff, however, is what makes her real. She made something fast, and her staff made it work. This is not a unique story, but it is a lovely moment that Adamson is eager to share. It is this kind of memory that pushes her to continue, even when she makes a mistake—it is most likely a story her students have heard many times when they face their own challenges. No one is perfect, but you learn to work with your team and your project in the best way you can. The ability and the desire to keep going is what is important, knowing that the next thing you make may be your favorite—on the dress form or off.

Adamson's pride in her own career history, as well as her place in the history of costume making, is evident: she tilts her chin up but cuts her eyes to mine with a smile after each story, emphasizing the wisdom she has gained from each of her experiences. As a teacher myself, it is her humor and retrospection that captivates me. Not only has Adamson established a long career in professional theatres like the Carolina Readers' Theatre, Alabama Shakespeare Theatre, and Utah Shakespeare Festival, she was the first head of Costume Technology for UNC Chapel Hill, a position developed to support the first graduate Costume Technology degree in the country associated with a professional theatre. While many university programs offer degrees in Costume Design, only a small percentage draw direct focus to the craft of costume making. After working for Matera in New York City, Millie Barringer, the department chair at UNC, asked her to return to Chapel Hill to teach costume technology, and after a year of commuting back and forth from NYC, she accepted a full-time position and began her academic career.

As someone who has spent her professional career in academia, I have a hard time imagining how one might leave a commercial shop to create an entirely a new academic program—yet, that's exactly what Adamson accomplished. As she herself states, she does not have an MFA, and she spent her previous time at Chapel Hill working in the costume shop, so the procedures and politics of higher education were far from her experience. Things like assessment, retention, and the broad structure of building a new curriculum were new to her. I asked her about how she went about the process herself.

IMAGE 3.7 *Fantasy Banker,* Crazy for You. *Designed By William Ivey Long. Constructed 1991, 1993, 1994 for Broadway, London, Toronto, and the National Tour.*
Photo courtesy of Judy Adamson.

"I started out staying one chapter ahead in the textbook from my students! When I knew I was gonna take the job, I took two flat patterning and a tailoring course at the Fashion Institute of Technology [FIT]. Not because *I* needed to know how to pattern, but I needed to understand the pace students learned the material in a classroom. And that was illuminating."

This distinction between professional and academic training is perhaps the most fascinating paradox in Adamson's life. She learned her skills in a professional studio, at the elbows of professional dressmakers, and she has found a way to translate those into a structured, highly regarded curriculum for her graduate students at Chapel Hill. Adamson took the time to consider the differences between how she learned and how her students would learn, and—in a very short time frame—integrated her skills with the ones she planned to teach her students. Every professor offers a combination of skills learned from their own time in the classroom and in professional studios, and many professors pass on those techniques the same way they were taught. Adamson, trained almost solely on the deadlines and expectations of a major Broadway costume shop, translated her own skills into one of the strongest curricula in the country.

IMAGE 3.8 *Third-year Costume Technology graduate students Rebecca Hyatt and Iisha Lemming try on corsets in in the workroom at the University of North Carolina at Chapel Hill, 2004.*
Photo courtesy of Judy Adamson.

I asked if there was something she wished she had learned before becoming an educator. "What do I wish that someone had taught me? I had no formal education, really. I felt my way though." Adamson described how she observed her teachers, how she reflected on her own experience in her FIT classes, and she used those experiences as models to inform the teaching of her students.

How did she build the program and recruit students? I asked. Adamson pointed back to the convention center. "At my first USITT, I overheard a conversation—somebody saying they had a student looking for a graduate school, and I interrupted and said I was looking for a graduate student. And that was Rosemary Ingham, and her student was Erica Malos. It got easier over time—students who came through go out and spread the word." Adamson's students are well known for the draping, cutting, and hand-sewing techniques she instills in them, and many have made their own impact in theatre departments and costume shops across the country. Many follow her footsteps to the costume shops of New York City, while others work at the Utah Shakespeare Festival, the Santa Fe Opera, the LA Opera, and graduate technology programs across the United States. Adamson focuses solely on costume technology—not just in her own work, but in her program recruitment and mentorship.

I have always been curious about that moment when a student realizes their calling. It's important for that student to have a mentor who can also recognize that, and empower that student's passion. I've seen many students nudged onto a design track despite their obvious inclinations for crafts or technology, and I was curious to know how Adamson negotiated that journey with her students. I quickly learned that for her, as the head of a graduate program, it was imperative that her students identify their own paths.

Out of curiosity, I asked if there was ever a time she saw a designer apply to her program and thought well, maybe . . .? Adamson quickly cut me off, both hands flat on the table. "No, you know what? I don't pay any attention to designers. They say they're a costume designer, I don't want 'em." Professionally, she works well with designers, but as an educator, she is in the business of training technicians, and she has spent many years fighting for costume technology to hold its own place on the professional stage. Technology and crafts have only recently gained their own competition and response categories in the Kennedy Center American College Theatre Festival, and the Southeastern Theatre Conference and USITT have just in the last few years listed these artisans separately in their job postings. Many small undergraduate programs emphasize design to the point of neglecting costume technology as a viable career field, when in fact the ratio of designers to technicians in most shops proves this wrong.

"Early on I interviewed a girl, asked her what she did when I was looking at her portfolio. 'What did you do in this picture?' I asked, and she said, 'Oh, the grunt work.' And I said, 'What does that mean?' and she said, 'Oh, I made them.' Well, she didn't get into my program. You have to have a respect for what you do, and what you contribute, to be a good collaborator."

Adamson describes the years she spent attending the Southeastern Theatre Conference, and how in the 1990s and early 2000s designers and technicians were grouped together for their interviews. "I insisted that they break it up so that the technicians were interviewed separately from designers. I really lobbied for that—and probably stepped on a lot of toes. But I demanded that costume technicians be given their own place. Now they've separated costume design from costume technology, and even costume crafts. I just hope it continues, you know."

This is no small thing. As the categories for national theatre job listings, interviews, and even academic competitions grow to include the wide variety of artisans, students are more likely to find—and find respect for—their technical skills and how these skills support their professional communities. Young technicians then begin to learn how they fit into the larger picture, and how integral their skills are to the process of design. It takes a lot of people and a lot of skills to bring full-scale designs to life onstage. Language matters, details and clarity matter for artisans and skilled laborers who work behind the scenes. Adamson's influence on her students and professional colleagues has had a significant impact on the workforce in academic theatre, which, in turn, has changed the workforce in professional costume shops. By recognizing costume technology as its own degree track, the skills of costumers and the costume curriculum have codified and evolved into higher standards for the profession. The position of draper or costume technician is elevated from "laborer" to skilled artisan, and along with that distinction comes standardized pay and a place in the hierarchy of the costume shop. A trained costume technician is distinctly different from a seamstress or home stitcher—not only in practice, but on paper.

IMAGE 3.9 *Judy Adamson sewing the tango dress for* The Cocoanuts, *Utah Shakespeare Festival. Designed by Bill Black, 2016.*
Photo courtesy of Judy Adamson.

That paper is evidence of a curriculum, a set of established techniques that standardize the profession. Costume shops filled with trained costume technologists set themselves apart from those without, and ultimately determine the definition of professionalism for the trade. Adamson sits with her hands linked together, eager to tell her own stories, but she believes firmly that costume technologists serve the design and the designer, and it is important to her that her students understand that dynamic. A professional draper must have great skills, but also a mentality that is creative and flexible so they can change along with the production and the design.

"Drapers have to let it go. They do their absolute best to take something in the fitting room that is the best they can do for the designer's vision, the best of their skill in terms of measurements and their interpretations of the sketch, but once they're in there, it's the designer's game, you know. It's the designer and actor who have to be served. And you can't have your feelings hurt. If you make a mistake, you admit to it and go on." This perspective is important but does not come easily to many artists. We want to hold onto our creations—and every small decision we made while making them—but ultimately that's not the point of what we do.

"You have to let it go because it's not you. You know one of the worst things is to work hours and hours and hours on something and then have it distressed. You get it back and go . . . oh! . . . you know? Or it's cut from the show, you've made this gorgeous dress and they just cut it."

As a designer, I have felt the pangs of regret over a piece that got cut from production, particularly when I consider the time and skill put into it. It's difficult, but it happens—and all too often once I see the entire show on stage I know that hard choice was the right one. Adamson wants to communicate that same awareness to her students: we have to love the details, but we also have to see the big picture. While we put a bit of ourselves into everything we make, ultimately we aren't making these things for ourselves, but for the audience's experience. I nodded in sympathy and asked her what makes her want to start again. Adamson smiled, tapping the table with two fingers. "I get that initial 'oomph' when I see the designs for the first time and get really intrigued, you know?

IMAGE 3.10 *Judy Adamson's team working on the Sugar Bowl for* Beauty and the Beast, *Barbara Matera's workroom, 1993.*
Photo courtesy of Judy Adamson.

I think 'I want to do that!' or 'That'll be fun to figure out!' That's always a good moment for me. I like to solve things, to figure out how something is done, how it goes together. That's one of the things a draper has to do. You can't drape well without knowing how things go together. I just love the process, I just love to sew. I don't get to do much of it anymore, but I love it. Even now, I always pick something that I can do myself."

When I asked if she likes to sew at home, she offered me wide eyes and tucked her chin into her neck: "Nooooo . . . ask my husband the last time I fixed any of his blue jeans . . . no I don't. I have a machine at home but I rarely use it. I have the shop—if I'm going to do something, I'll do it in the shop." Adamson's love for the craft showed through as she spoke, but it is clear that her craft has migrated permanently into her work life. Sewing is such a helpful skill to have—professionally and as a hobby—but I can tell her passion is really about what happens in the costume shop.

What are the main skills she thinks a technician should have, I asked. "I think curiosity of how things are done is one of the main virtues. You know, I want to try that, I want to get my hands in that . . . that's a real virtue. I don't have time for the kid that says 'I know how to do that!' Because they don't; they might think they do, but they don't know the beginning. You want the adventuresome, curious student. They're going to dabble, they're going to create, and you know . . ."

I finished her sentence, ". . . maybe find that thing they love desperately." She agreed. "Yeah! Right! I don't believe there's a right way to put something together. There are a lot of ways to make something, but some of them are better than others."

She continued. "I also talk to my students all the time about how they're holding their tools and the way they're working and what they're doing to their bodies. You've got to learn to protect yourself and your work. I like to see people who sew with a thimble. I don't think you're serious unless you have a thimble on your finger. If you joined a group of sewing ladies basting a hem up at Matera's and you weren't sewing in the right direction with a thimble on your finger, they'd just tell you to get out because they don't have time to work around you. It's a symbol of how earnest you are about doing it and doing it quickly. If you're always worried about whether or not you're going to hurt your finger, you're not thinking about the job. And it's not fast. You can't be fast if you don't have a thimble."

Adamson's attention to tools and work practices demonstrates her awareness of the ways in which our work patterns not only impact our bodies but also the quality of the finished product. Like many students today, I wasn't taught to sew with a thimble. But since my conversation with Adamson, I have acquired and fallen in love with my leather thimble and taken to heart what this tool says about my work. Many students aren't taught to sew with a thimble, and it often isn't until they start working with leather that such a tool seems needed—at which point many pick up a pair of pliers to pull the needle through instead. Those pliers usually bend or break the needle, and without fail compress the needle's eye—which leads to broken or shredded thread. The proper use of one small tool, a thimble, therefore affects all the other tools a technician works with.

When I asked Adamson if there are any new technologies she's attracted to, she once

IMAGE 3.11 *Judy Adamson sewing on mermaid frills for* Peter and the Starcatcher. *Costume design by Holly Poe Durbin.*
Photo courtesy of Judy Adamson.

again rubbed her thumbs together over her clasped hands. "You still use scissors, you still use thread, you still use sewing machines . . . I suppose the importance on safety is one of the really big things. That's just gotten so much better and it's all for the good." In 1986, OSHA (Occupational Safety and Health Administration) began requiring Material Safety Data Sheets (MSDS) for all hazardous materials. The ways artisans handle many materials and chemicals have changed dramatically in the last 30 years. The expanse of paint, dye, and coloring mediums available, in addition to the profusion of thermoplastics, make this kind of information integral to technologists and craft artisans alike. However these aren't the only technological changes Adamson considers significant.

"In terms of 3D printing, digital printing . . . I appreciate all that, I really do. I think it has a real place in what we do. I taught computer patterning for a few years, although I didn't personally find it satisfying, and I don't think the students really did either. They can pick it up faster than I can teach it anyway. I appreciate all of it but I also realize that it is going to go a long way without me." Adamson plans to retire in July 2019, and admitted that her feelings about technology come from the reality that she will not be using most of it herself. She has had fabrics digitally printed, and she has "fiddled" with many of the newer tools, but she admits that she happily returns to her needle and thimble even on her best day.

Adamson has been an advocate for costume technologists and artisans for the last twenty years, and her advocacy has led to great changes in academic structures, professional titles, and industrywide standards for the field. While she may laugh at how she stumbled into the industry, her skills and her perspectives speak to her success, as they have for decades. One imagines that even as she smiles at the thought of retirement, Adamson will still keep her hands busy, and keep her eyes out for her students for years to come.

ARTIST BIO

Judy Adamson has been the Costume Director for PlayMakers Repertory Company and Head of the Costume Production program in the Department of Dramatic Art at the University of North Carolina since 1993. Before coming to North Carolina, Judy worked for fourteen years at Barbara Matera Ltd., one of the foremost costume houses in New York. She was Barbara's assistant and workroom manager until 1990 when she began draping for the company. She has draped clothes for Broadway shows such as *Crazy for You*, *Jelly's Last Jam*, *The Secret Garden*, *Showboat*, *Moon Over Buffalo*, *Hairspray*, *Flower Drum Song*, *Sideshow*, and Disney's *Beauty and the Beast*, worked with designers such as Irene Sharaff, Miles White, Theoni Aldredge, Florence Klotz, Patricia Zipprodt, William Ivey Long, and Bob Mackie.

Judy has also worked extensively in dance with the American Ballet Theatre, Paul Taylor, and Elliot Feld. Judy and her students have worked on productions such as *Coppelia*, *Carmen*, *Great Galloping Gottschalk*, *Messiah*, and *Picnic in the Garden* for Carolina Ballet, the Raleigh-based dance company.

As well as draping for PlayMakers Repertory Company, Judy is in the process of reorganizing and documenting the vintage collection in the Department of Dramatic Art with the help of undergraduate work-study students. Each garment is being documented with a photograph and description. The garments are of interest to all costume students, but the hope is that the information will be useful across disciplines with access through **costumes.unc.edu/costar/.**

Judy has compiled information on costume programs throughout the country for United States Institute for Theatre Technology (USITT) called Survey of Costume Programs in the United States. The survey, edited each fall, can be found under related links at **http://costume-survey.info**. Judy has co-edited *Projects for Teaching Costume Design and Technology, Volume 2* for USITT as well.

Judy has draped at the Utah Shakespeare Festival in Cedar City, Utah, for the past thirteen summers: *Hay Fever* and *Anything Goes* (designed by Kevin Alberts), *Born Yesterday*, *Mornings at Seven*, *A Midsummer Night's Dream*, *HMS Pinafore*, *Lend Me a Tenor, The Musical*, *Two Gentlemen of Verona*, *Foxfire*, *Noises Off!*, and *Pride and Prejudice* (designed by Bill Black), *Private Lives*, *The Glass Menagerie*, and *Scapin* (designed by David Mickelsen), and *Sense and Sensibility* (designed by Holly Payne).

Source: http://drama.unc.edu/faculty-member/judy-adamson/

CHAPTER 4

MARGARET PEOT, COSTUME PAINTER

Christin Essin

IMAGE 4.1 *Margaret Peot, costume painter at Parsons-Mears, LTD and member of IATSE Local 829.* Photo by David Perlman.

On June 5, 2015, I met with costume painter Margaret Peot at New York City's Cornelia Street Café; she had suggested the location because it is an easy commute from the Parsons-Meares costume shop in Long Island City. It has also been a favorite haunt of Peot's since she arrived in the city in 1986, and the owner (now a friend), Robin Hirsch, had previously hosted a group show at the location called the "Art of Costume Painting." The café's walls featured a series of painted samples from the work of Parsons-Meares's painters, including Peot, Welles-Tolkan, Virginia Clow, Claudia Dzundza, and Mary Macy. The challenge of costume painting, according to the "brief history" written by Welles-Tolkan and Peot to accompany the samples, "is finding the method and paint medium that satisfied the designer's vision and withstands the rigors of eight shows a week for a lengthy run . . . From the designer's concept, to what one ultimately sees on the stage, costume painting is often the most elegant solution" to helping the designer "fully realize the costume he or she drew."[1] Once we ordered lunch, Peot handed me a copy of her book *Stencil Craft* (2015), a how-to manual that demonstrates for the layperson some of the fabric painting techniques she has perfected during the more than twenty-five years she has worked at Parsons-Mears.

Owned and run by Sally Ann Parsons, Parsons-Meares is one of New York's premiere costume shops; it began serving the theatre industry in 1980 and soon became known for its excellence in craft work after securing a contract to construct costumes for the musical *Cats* (1982).[2] The Broadway production "demanded different methods of applying paint to satisfy the vision of the costume designer, John Napier," the exhibit history explained, so Parsons outfitted her shop with four to five full-time costume painters to meet the growing demand for their techniques. Over the years, Peot and Parsons-Meares's costume painters have crafted costumes for a number of high-profile Broadway musicals such as *Phantom of the Opera*, *The Lion King*, and *Wicked*; renowned dance companies such as the Joffrey Ballet and the Alvin Ailey American Dance Theatre; and a variety of live entertainments such as Disney on Ice and Ringling Brothers Barnum and Bailey Circus.

Peot moved to New York City in the 1980s after graduating with a studio art degree from Miami University of Ohio. "I always had been able to make money working in the theatre to support my studio work. I designed posters for productions, painted scenery for community theatres, lots of stuff." Once she arrived, Peot picked up work as a scenic painter with Bruce and Bruce, a nonunion shop, and then some work for Parsons-Meares as a fabric dyer.

While Peot loved the shop and its employees, dying is "very hard work," she recalled, "really stressful, really hot, and there was no air-conditioning back in the day." She took a break from Parsons to work for a mural painting shop owned by two members of the United Scenic Artists (USA) union, now known as Local 829 of the International Alliance of Theatrical Stage Employees (IATSE). Reflecting back, she said, "Painting murals and theatrical scenery helped me to become a good costume painter because it's the same deal. Everything has to look great from a distance. Something that looks really perfect from the audience may not look like anything close up. So, that's served me very well." Peot later became a member of USA, not as a scenic painter but as part of the smaller Allied Crafts section based on her costume work.

Parsons later asked Peot to return to the shop as a costume painter; the company had expanded, moved locations, and secured contracts with companies outside the New York area, providing costumes for theme parks, touring ice skating shows, and other types of spectacular productions. "But I said no—never—because I just assumed it would be the same thing as being a dyer, physically difficult and super high stress. But then all of the other painters who worked there, who had started there, called me individually to tell me how great they thought I was for the job and how much fun we would have." At the time, Parsons specifically needed more painters to complete their contract for a Siegfried and Roy production in Las Vegas. "The show had forty showgirls with different costumes for each scene. They were butterflies in one, flowers in another, then tiger people, and they all needed to be painted. So, I decided I would do it, but just for that show. Then I was outta there!"

Except she wasn't.

Peot has stayed with Parsons, continuing to refine her skills as part of the tight-knit team that includes Macy, Clow, and Tolkan; they were sad to lose Dzundza, who passed away in 2013. "Even though I've been there for almost twenty-five years, I'm still the new girl, the baby. It's a family, really. We're like sisters." When the shop moved to its current location in Long Island City, Parsons set the painters up in the corner of the shop "with the best light" and "two walls of windows" so they can see clearly for painting detail and mixing colors.

Once we finished lunch, I began to ask Peot more specific questions about her work and the skills required for costume painting.

CE: I took a brief tour through Parsons-Meares a few days ago, and it looks like a great place to work. A lot of people who work in the theatre talk about their co-workers as a family, but there's a difference between those who connect in a performance venue and those who connect around the work in shops.

MP: Yeah, I'm not one of those people who thrive off the intensity of performances, having this one intense experience and then having it end and moving on to the next intense experience. I like the continuity of our shop and being around the people I love. Sally Ann is remarkable, unbelievably kind, and the smartest person I've ever met. She's been an incredible mentor, and she looks out for us. Designers also appreciate her contagious enthusiasm and wealth of ideas; whenever they walk into the shop with a new sketch, she begins spinning ideas about how the design can be realized. So, the work I get to do is interesting and fun . . . seductive, really, because it is work that engages your whole mind. As an artist, I want to work for someone who is a collaborator, and that's Sally Ann and her staff.

CE: What kind of skill set do you need to work as a costume painter?

MP: Skill set . . . hmmm. [*She pauses to think.*] Well, all the basic scenic painting skills, sponging, spattering, all those things we use to create texture, the use of stencils . . .

CE: Do you ever paint at a distance, like scenic painters with brushes extended on poles?

MP: No . . . it's tricky. Our surfaces are smaller. We're painting on clothes, not a giant piece of scenery. We actually *have* to paint it close up, stretched out flat on a table. Our paint is a dye mixed in a gelatinous base, so when you're painting, it doesn't have the same value or vibrancy that it will have after it's been processed. So, we create a lot of samples to experiment with different ideas, and we have to remember, hold in our mind, what it is *going* to look like rather than what we see while we're painting it. That's the tricky part.

CE: So the paint you use is manufactured specifically for fabric?

MP: Yes, by Gene Mignola.[3] The paint and method we use started with Willa Kim [*Tony Award–winning costume designer*]. She was designing for the Joffrey Ballet Company and was working with Ray Diffin's costume shop. [*Earlier in her career, Parsons worked as a draper for Diffin.*] Willa wanted painted dance costumes, something that could look like Léon

IMAGE 4.2 *Poet painting a flying monkey costume for the Broadway musical* Wicked. Photo by Peter Clough.

Bakst's designs without any kind of clunky paint with texture. She wanted them to be like bathing suits with perfectly vibrant colors and perfectly fit to the performer's body. She did some research on people who silk screened on bathing suits. And she found this guy out in Queens who was willing to make her some paint. The dye that we paint with soaks into the fabric and then it is steam set. Once it's set, it's washable and there's no feeling of paint, just the fabric. Now Gene makes all of our paint; it's more uniform in color, more stable, and has a longer shelf life than what Willa started with.

[She begins to pull samples she brought out of a bag.]

I brought all of these because they really show the collaborative nature of the work. Every single show that comes into the shop has its own set of problems and fun things to figure out.

Now that I think about it, maybe the most important skill for a costume painter is being able to duplicate an approved sample, and also being able to repeat the process on costumes that are reordered for a long-running production, making sure that the designer's vision is replicated and there is continuity throughout the run of a show. So record keeping is important, too.

So, for example, here's an approved sample for the Pinocchio costume from *Shrek: The Musical*. We had a lot of samples before this one—some were very ugly—from when we were trying to work out the wood-graining effect. Wood graining for scenery is easy because you use a tool that takes paint away, leaving some color behind in a woodgrain pattern. But figuring out how to do it on a piece of fabric is trickier because as soon as you put the paint down, there is no way to pull it out. You have to think about it in reverse, like a watercolor painting. The first samples were really ugly, but we experimented with different things, and finally settled on a look that the designer liked. But I have a whole box of wood-graining samples from just to try to figure out how to make it look nice from a distance. With one sample, I might get the technique right, but the fabric wouldn't look enough like wood. This sample, on wool felt, was just right—the colors were rich

IMAGE 4.3 *Pinocchio pants detail for* Shrek: The Musical. *Painted by Margaret Peot. Designed by Tim Hatley.* Photo courtesy of Margaret Peot.

enough, the fabric with its layers—that was Sally Ann's idea—was matte and also stiff like wood. It answered the folkloric feel the designer [*Tim Hatley*] was after.

[*The next sample appears.*]

This piece is one of many mermaid tail samples that I painted for Bette Midler's *The Showgirl Must Go On* [*designed by Constance Hoffman*]. I think this one was rejected because the colors were too dreary. The most spectacular mermaid costume for that show, in my opinion, was hot pink, but there was another black one with scales that had hints of copper and verdigris, and another that was lobster red.

IMAGE 4.4 *Peot with sample at the Cornelia Street Café.*
Photo courtesy of Margaret Peot.

CE: How do you get such clean lines?

MP: Well, I will tell you, and then you can do it at home! [*Peot points to my new* Stencil Craft *book, and we laugh.*] You make a stencil with a piece of plastic, or stencil Mylar, by cutting out a row of scale shapes. Then you . . . let me think a minute [*she picks up feels the fabric, remembering her process*] . . . you paint off the edge of the stencil, then move it and paint off the edge again, and again, using this murky green color, see? Then you take a brush with an almond shaped end—a filbert—and go [*showing me*]—bloop, bloop, bloop—with each of the different colors.

CE: Are those sparkles glued on?

MP: They are hot press stones. We set the crystals in a transfer machine so they get really, really hot. Once they are set, you can wash them.

[*Next, she shows me a sample on a soft, stretchable fabric used to create the illusion of a tattooed arm.*]

We made this to match the performer's flesh tone. It wasn't meant to be realistic, more of a fantasy tattoo. The colors are high key, and we painted in more white areas, which is not typical of real tattoos, so that the audience could see the detail at a distance.

CE: So, the samples are a big part of the process, and with each new project or material you just start playing and figuring out what is possible . . .

MP: Oh yeah . . . that's what most of these all are. Rejected samples. Designers provide sketches and research to help the painter start the sample process. The painter imagines how to translate the sketch into full-scale reality and then creates a sample to explain her solution to the costume designer. The dialogue with the designer starts with a single sample that initiates reaction and questions on the part of the designer. Some projects can be solved with only one sample, but it is more usual to go through several steps. We also use samples to test for durability, or a draper might use them to test different appliques, beading, or stitch finishes.

For one of our recent projects, *King Arthur* at the Cincinnati Ballet, we worked with Sandra Woodall [*designer*] to create costumes with wool felting. They paid us to experiment; we had never worked with wool felting, and initially felt sure we could figure out a technique that looks like wool felting without being actual wool felting. We tried, but we couldn't. And since Woodall wanted it to be wool felting, we learned to do wool felting. So now I'm really enjoying it . . . it's an unbelievably cool process!

We achieved this cross-hatching effect with the use of squeeze bottles and stencils . . . we use a lot of squeeze

IMAGES 4.5 AND 4.6 *Costume for* King Arthur's Camelot, *2014 premiere. Choreographed by Victoria Morgan for the Cincinnati Ballet. Designed by Sandra Woodall.*

IMAGE 4.7 *Sample for* Starlight Express on Ice. *Painted by Margaret Peot. Designed by Frank Krenz.* Photo courtesy of Margaret Peot.

bottles. We apply with brushes, airbrushing, natural sponges, silk screens, rollers, or even a feather.

[*She pulls out another sample.*]

This we made for an Iron Man costume. If I showed this to anyone who didn't know anything about theatre, they'd say, "Well, what did you paint? It's just a shiny thing." But, in fact, all of the shine and gleam, all of the shadows were airbrushed.

Once when I was working with Willa on a ballet, the women's costumes were painted in earthy colors with puffy, cloudlike sleeves. I was so proud of what I was doing, so I invited my husband to the shop to show him. And I could see that he was not impressed! All he saw were these giant zippers and big snaps that stood out—dance companies use costumes for years, so they have to be hefty. But then he went to see the show, and they looked ethereal, beautiful! You couldn't see the zippers or snaps or pieces of Velcro or whatever . . . they just looked like magic. Which is, of course, the whole point.

[*She returns to the Iron Man sample.*]

We accomplished all of the texture for this costume with paint on flexible

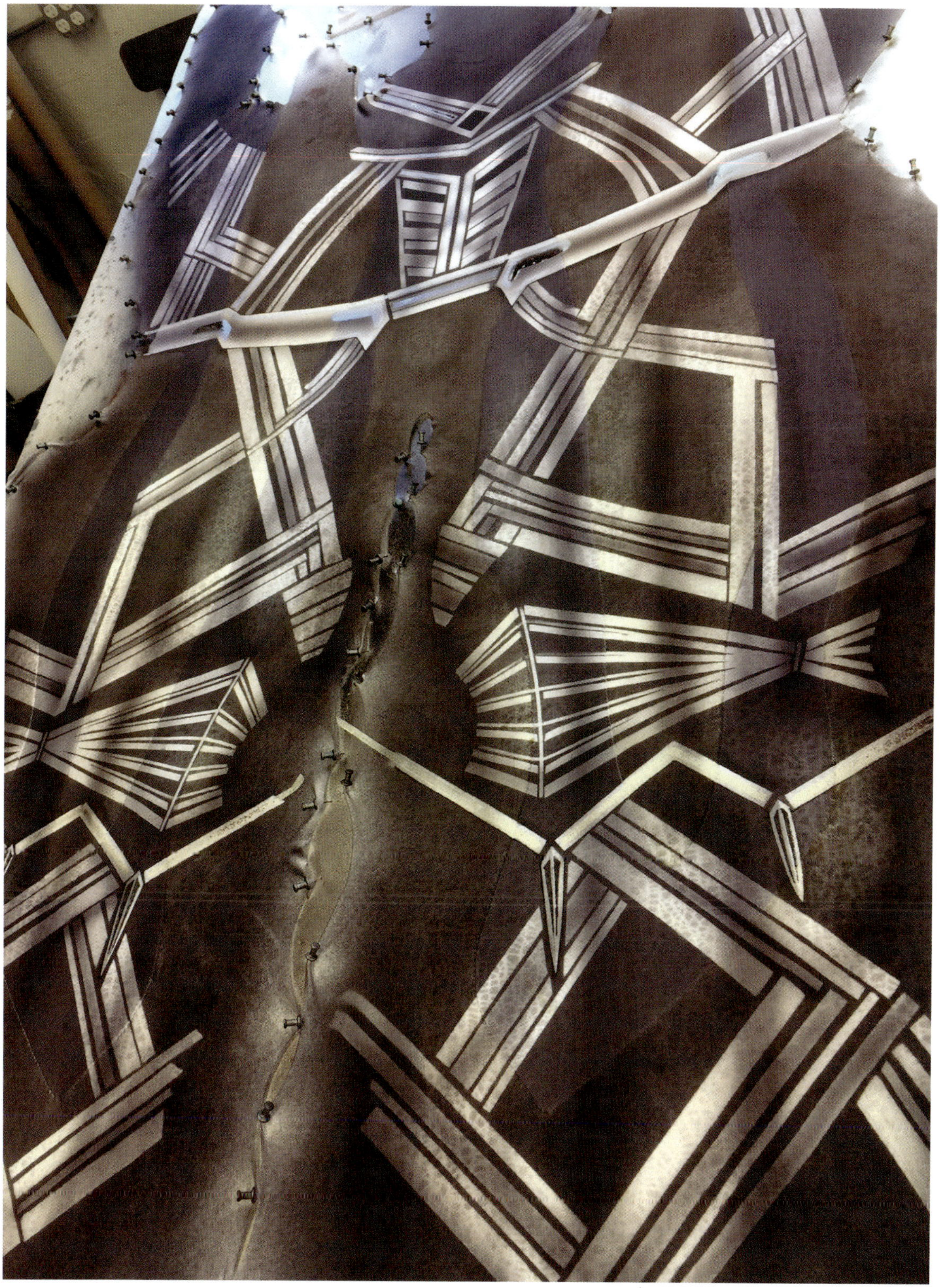

IMAGE 4.8 *Marvel costume detail. Painted by Margaret Peot. Designed by Mark Koss.*
Photo courtesy of Margaret Peot.

materials so that the costume would look like hard metal and also be light, pliable, and breathable for the performer. It's a stunt show, and at a certain point the performer has to lift his arm up around and hook himself to a flying rig, so nothing can get in his way.

CE: Right, it has to work on stage . . .

MP: Yes. What it looks like is of identical importance to how it functions. They go hand in hand. Plus, everything we do has to be able to be laundered, to has to be durable . . .

CE: . . . it has to be sweated in eight times a week.

MP: Exactly.

CE: So, the production really relies on you because applique is not always functional.

MP: Right. But also, applique is often really expensive. If you have twenty things to create, it's too much. Especially if I can just do it with a stencil.

CE: How have new technologies in digital printing changed what you do?

MP: I knew you were going to ask me about that. Yes.

For some projects, I know in advance that a lot of the fabric will be digitally printed. So, I create artwork rather than painting directly on each costume. That artwork becomes digitalized and printed on fabric. The Disney theme parks, for example, hired us to create costumes for Tinkerbell and her flower fairy friends . . . I can't remember their names, but there's a yellow one, blue one, red, orange, purple. There's also bad girl. Anyway, we couldn't possibly paint forty Tinkerbell costumes, and forty of the next and the next for all of the performers walking around all of their parks. So, I painted samples on woven silk, and we shipped them to California where they digitalized the design and printed it on stretch fabric.

It's a wonderful technology, but even before digital printing, we mass-produced painted fabric with silk screening. For one of the ice shows, we worked with Gene [*Mignola*] to create a large number of costumes with evil bat wings; he silk-screened all the wings with a swirling design and sent them back to us to add more detail.

Now Gene does a lot more digital printing. We collaborated on the Wolverine [*from the X-Men*] costume for one of the Marvel Universe stunt shows. I painted the musculature and shading in black and white on a unitard pattern, and then he scanned the pattern. For each, he could move the musculature around for fit while also integrating the different colors and textures. He's a wonderful printer with a great artistic eye, and we have lots of experience airbrush painting anatomically correct musculature for all of our *Lion King* guys. So, it's a great collaboration.

More recently, we worked together on some ostrich costumes for Radio City Music Hall's Spring Spectacular. Gene digitally printed the fabric, and we added the feather artwork. I suppose before digital printing we would have just divided the work up between the four of us. But we would have been out of our minds busy if we had to paint all of those feather dresses, and producers aren't paying as much as they used to . . . I mean, before, with a show like *The Will Rogers Follies* [*1991*], we painted everything. There were twenty showgirls, and Willa designed distinct costumes for each one; each had a pair of chaps with cow spots in different places. So, if we had had digital printing, would she have settled for something more uniform? Probably not. She was very particular about the color and sheen, and with digital printing you aren't always able to get your top choice of fabric. But producers aren't spending that kind of money now. Nobody would ever recreate that parade of jeweled dresses it would be so expensive. Nobody spends money like that anymore.

Really, we are just starting to see the influence of digital printing. But does it have its limits?

It's interesting [*she pulls out another sample*] . . . this is something else I painted for Disney, a costume for the character Helen in *The Incredibles*, daywear, not her superhero outfit. I taped off this part and waxed it . . .

CE: You painted with wax?

MP: Yeah, heated it up and painted with it. The wax offers resistance to the color. The designer didn't want a crisp look, but something murkier, a watery effect. I mean, maybe you could get that with digital printing, but I'm not sure . . . it would be harsher, I think.

[*We spend a few minutes flipping through* Stencil Craft, *with Peot pointing out certain techniques used in the samples we discussed. The book is only one of a series of publishing projects that fill out her work as a freelance artist.*]

CE: It's great that you have documented all of these techniques. And I really appreciate you sitting down with me today to discuss your work.

MP: I was flattered to be asked! Although, I do think it's really important that people know what we do. There are a lot of younger artists coming into the costume industry, but mostly as first-hands and drapers. We need more costume painters; it's an art that's dying out, and we don't want it to lose it.

CE: Do you ever teach costume painting?

MP: Yes, I used to co-teach costume painting at NYU's Tisch School of the Arts with Mary Macy for nine to ten years. And I have given workshops in costume painting at USITT-SE [*United States Institute for Theatre Technology, Southeast Conference*], Miami University, and Brigham Young University. I also worked with Rachel E. Pollock at the University of North Carolina at Chapel Hill.[4] She worked for Parsons-Meares on *Shrek*, I think. At the time, I didn't know she was a teacher, but I met her again at the USITT-SE workshop, and she asked me to visit the UNC costume production program and teach a painting class. I had another book coming out called *The Successful Artist's Career Guide*, which is

IMAGE 4.9 *Sample created with wax resist, stencils, and squeeze-bottle lines for Ringling Brothers Barnum and Bailey Circus. Painted by Margaret Peot. Designed by Frank Krenz.*
Photo courtesy of Margaret Peot.

about how to make a living as an artist, so I also did a talk about that.

CE: So many of my students need that!

MP: I interviewed people like me who live in the real world as artists. It's a book I wish someone had given me when I was a kid getting out of college.

After interviewing Peot, I read *The Successful Artist's Career Guide* and quickly gave my copy to a student. The book not only offers practical advice but also encourages readers to chart their life and career path with the same enthusiasm and dedication they give their artistry. Like *Stencil Craft*, it is a how-to guide, but it also speaks to Peot's long, successful career as an artist who has made the most out of the opportunities that have come her way, remaining curious and open to new techniques and technologies. "You don't have to be what others think an artist should be," she tells her readers.[5] Peot followed her own path and found a rewarding career as a costume painter, carving out a niche within the theatre industry where she can thrive and continue to build her skill set.

ARTIST BIO

From Peot's website: www.margaretpeot.com

My mother told me that when I was a little girl I told her that I was going to be an artist until I was 35 years old, and then be a writer. I don't remember telling her this, but it's kind of what happened. And happily, becoming a writer didn't preclude being an artist! I have written and illustrated several books for both kids and adults. I have illustrated three paper toy sets for Pomegranate Publishing, including the *NEW FAIRY HOUSE: A Color, Punch Out and Play Set*, *MUSEUM VISIT: A Color, Punch Out and Play Set*, and *TEA PARTY: A Color, Punch Out and Play Set*. My first coloring book, *Let's Color Together: A Shareable Coloring Book for Parents and Kids*, came out this spring from Sourcebooks, and was followed by a "sequel," *Let's Color Together: SECRET WORLDS: A Shareable Coloring Book for Parents and Kids*. Other titles include *Stencil Craft: Techniques for Art, Fashion and Home* (F&W) and *Crow Made a Friend* (Holiday House), an early reader picture book and finalist in the 2016 Ohioana Awards for juvenile literature. *Inkblot: Drip, Splat and Squish Your Way to Creativity* (Boyds Mills, 2011) was awarded a Eureka! Silver Medal for nonfiction children's books. Also, *The Successful Artist's Career Guide: Finding Your Way in the Business of Art* (F&W, 2012) is used in high school and college counseling offices to guide people who want to have a career as an artist. I've also published *Alternative Art Journals: Explore Innovative Approaches to Collecting Your Creativity* (F&W 2012), and *Make Your Mark: Explore Your Creativity and Discover Your Inner Artist* (Chronicle Books, 2004), which was voted one of *Library Journal*'s best how-to books of 2004. I am represented by literary agent Anna Olswanger.

I have had the great good fortune to be able to support my drawing and writing activities over the past 20+ years by painting and dying costumes for the theatre at Parsons-Meares, LTD. The theatre has been a generous benefactor, and I am grateful every day for the chance to collaborate with such fantastic artists and artisans. I have painted on a hundred projects, certainly, including Broadway shows such as *Aladdin*, *The Lion King*, *Wicked*, *Turn Off the Dark*, *Will Rogers Follies*, *Shrek the Musical*, *Phantom of the Opera*, and *Mary Poppins*, and dance performances such as the American Ballet Theater's *Peter and the Wolf*, the Joffrey Ballet's *Cotillon* and *Pilobolus*, the Feld Ballet's *Evo and Paper Tiger*, and the Nevada Ballet's and San Francisco Ballet's *Nutcrackers*. I also worked on the film *Bram Stoker's Dracula*, as well as for circuses, arena shows, and ice shows. I am a proud and long-time member of United Scenic Artists, Local 829.

I teach costume painting (NYU's Tisch School of the Arts, University of North Carolina [UNC], Brigham Young University [BYU], USITT-SE) and present lectures on making a living as an artist (the Self Employment in the Arts 2013 conference in Chicago; the Love Your Library series at FIT; Miami University in Ohio; BYU; UNC). I present art workshops (Inkblots, Invisible Ink, Stencils, other) with cancer survivors, elders, children, parent and teen groups, writers, nurses, and caregivers at the Creative Center at University Settlement's Creative Aging conferences and their Artist-in-Residence Training program, with EngAGE Utah, at Gilda's Club, the Huntsman Cancer Institute, Operation Exodus in New York City, at Miami University's Scripps Center with Dr. Like Lokon, Opening Minds Through Art, and the Art Lab at Mount Sinai Hospital with Robin Glazer at The Creative Center.

I attended Miami University in Oxford, Ohio, and studied with Alex McKibben, Rocio Rodriguez, Lon Beck, Thomas Effler, Geoff Fishburn, Michael Griffiths, and Crossan Curry. I am pleased and honored to be serving on the first College of Creative Arts Advisory Board at Miami.

NOTES

1. Peot, Margaret. "On Stages/In Stages: The Art of Costume Painting—Parsons Meares, Ltd." (September 1–30, 2011). Unpublished.
2. Morris, Triffin, and Gregory D. L. Morris. "The History of the Broadway Costume Business." *Theatre Design & Technology* (2011) 47, no. 1: 10–19.
3. For more information on Gene Mignola, see "In the Wings," American Theatre Wing, RPP Productions (2016). https://vimeo.com/192249460.
4. My thanks to Rachel Pollock for connecting me with Peot and helping make this interview possible.
5. Peot, Margaret. *The Successful Artist's Career Guide: Finding Your Way in the Business of Art*. (Cincinnati, OH: North Light Books, 2012).

CHAPTER 5

MAKING SHAKESPEARE IN MONTANA

Tom Watson, Scenic Artist

Courtney Smith

IMAGE 5.1 *Scenic artist Tom Watson at his studio.*
Photo courtesy of Tom Watson.

At any moment, Tom Watson can pull out a skill from his back pocket. He is a true theatre maker—a "Swiss army knife" in the allied arts. In a field that is ever-changing from project to project, moment to moment, audience to audience—the best strategy for a scenic artist is to let such a statement be narrative in its form and biographical in its content. A friend and colleague once told me that story is a major currency of theatre, so it's an effective tool in discussing how somebody makes it.

Like everyone in theatre, Tom loves a good story. Since the earliest human civilizations, theatre has been integral to the fabric of human communication. Theatre is rooted in Western tradition and part of a broader culture of festivals and religious rituals. Our ancestors sat around campfires trading stories about *The Iliad*. Homer performed these epic poems in song and speech. The sacred texts of the Bible and Quran serve as guidebooks to religions. But far from instruction manuals, they are detailed morality stories passed along by storytellers and performed as liturgical dramas. Many believe that Shakespeare's folio was transcribed long after the work was first performed. A story is a logical way to begin a discussion of anybody's work in the theatre. It is more than anecdotally interesting to start Tom's story at the very beginning.

THE EARLY YEARS

Born in Denver, Colorado, Tom grew up in the suburbs of Denver. Both his parents had studied theatre in college and often exposed all their kids to the arts. As a family they would go to professional touring shows, as well as local venues, as often as possible. The work ethic and the sense of play Tom learned in these early and sincere experiences cannot be discounted as sentimentality alone; they have had an honest impact on his work and laid a strong foundation for his first efforts as a theatre maker. At the young age of seven, Tom took acting classes at The Bonfils Theatre in downtown Denver. Instead of typical playground games, Tom was known around the neighborhood as the kid that created puppet shows, plays, and musicals with his friends. His activities during the school day were populated with theatre, choir, band, studio art, and anything else that was craft oriented or performance driven.

Tom's interest in theatre began in the way it does for most kids who get bit by the acting bug. While he says being on stage seemed like fun, it was other craft elements of theatre—design and scenic art—that quickly caught his attention. As a youth Tom was always interested in the arts. It was through art that he realized the key to transforming emotion. He is not defined by what he creates but is grateful to be a tool that channels divine energy into manifested form. In his element, he creates not only artwork but also joy that spreads to all those around. This joy infects every person he works with. When Tom was eighteen years old, and a recent high school graduate, he went to visit a summer theatre production of *Picnic* by William Inge and was overwhelmed by the scenic elements as he sat in the theatre prior to curtain. The illusion of the naturalistic environment of two back porches and shared backyard area was so convincing to Tom that he wondered how they had moved a few 1950s homes onto the stage. As he began to scan his program to find this information, the lighting designer had created a slow preshow sunrise effect in harmony with a sound design of birds waking from the dark evening into early morning. As he experienced this lifelike theatrical illusion from his comfortably padded assigned seat, his jaw dropped more and more. This level of amazement was prior to the performance even beginning. It was that moment that made Tom want to start his training to be a part of this amazing creative craft.

LEARNING THE CRAFT

Throughout his career Tom has been fortunate to have access to great teachers. Through them, he has found guidance in developing his craft. The best teachers had at least one thing in common: they always gave him the opportunity and support to reach out and try and accomplish a new goal or achieve something beyond his comfort level.

Tom's first significant mentor was Bruce Brockman, a scenic design professor at the University of Idaho. Today Bruce is a professor at the School of Theatre, Film and Television at the University of Arizona. Bruce introduced him to all the fundamentals of design and scenic painting and first inspired him to think of pursuing theatre crafts. It was at this time that he learned the elements and principles of design and started looking at objects and space in a different manner. As an acting student in an undergraduate theatre department, Tom was given an opportunity to design the set for a student production of *Androcles and the Lion*. Although this was not the point that he decided to move away from performance and into theatre craft and artistry, it was a significant moment in that he discovered that he not only had a knack for it, but that it was highly rewarding. "I worked in a shop during my time in Moscow," he said. "I got to acquire a real taste and respect for the work." Tom's experiences at the University of Idaho led him to pursue his MFA at the University of Nebraska–Lincoln in Design and Technical Theatre. "Tom was a wonderful student and a true theatre artist. He was a fine actor, had real talent as a visual artist and artisan, and was passionate about the community of collaborative storytelling. While the glamor of design and production never quite matches that of performers there is a joy that comes from collective creativity that feeds stage designers and artisans. Tom's success and artistic accomplishments certainly point to a career that has been deeply satisfying for him. I am proud to have played a small role in his story," Bruce said on his time spent with Tom.

IMAGES 5.2 AND 5.3 Twelfth Night *backdrop panels in process and final. Montana Shakespeare in the Schools; tour 2017.*
Photo courtesy of Tom Watson.

Tom had many mentors at the graduate level that helped shape his craft and sense of theatre-making, including Ed Stauffer and Chuck O'Conner from University of Nebraska–Lincoln. He will never forget fellow grad student Rob McKercher, a directing candidate who had spent a career in New York as a professional charge artist for more than a decade. He had been the charge on Broadway, television (*Saturday Night Live*), and significant feature films. Of the thirty-seven Broadway productions painted, Rob was the charge artist on *Secret Garden*, which won the 1991 Tony Award for Best Scenic Design by Heidi Landesman-Ettinger. He helped Tom with some of his design work and took Tom's painting artistry to a new level. He spoke about layers of color and creating three-dimensional color as a scenic artist. Although these techniques were not too far from techniques Tom had been taught and already using, it was more about how he explained these concepts to him in a way that made many light bulbs turn on for him. Rob helped Tom refine his execution of these ideas. He asked Tom to look around at the world, which enlightened his perception to see layers of color in real-world environments and materials. "We, as people, used to do a lot more active observation. We used to observe artwork as though it was a major story time. I tell all my students to look at the world as though they're seeing it for the first time," he says. It's easy to lose the sense of storytelling in an age of social media and tiny computers in your pocket but Tom hopes to encourage everyone to look with wonder. "Tom has a unique curiosity to explore and mine the depths within his incredible designs finding the nuances in color and shape that bring the text of the playwright to life. Every theatre artist seeks to find a universal beauty in their work, and Tom's impeccable work is no exception," says Rob, reflecting on his time with Tom. His experiences with Rob and at the University of Nebraska–Lincoln made it clear to him how colors could layer upon other colors in many situations. It was this visual epiphany that changed Tom's craft as he started to improve his use of glazes and translucent painting techniques and pushed beyond the way he was painting prior to this mentorship.

POSTGRAD LIFE

Tom's first job in theatre is difficult to pinpoint because his own process of paying dues and getting opportunities in academic theatre was a lengthy path of climbing the career ladder. His career path to become a scenic artist was built on taking jobs whenever and wherever he could—as general shop help, production assistant, run crew, and artistic craftsperson in academic productions. His first significant job was for a seasonal summer theatre company in southern Kansas where he was hired to help with some technical direction for one of the season's first shows. Once he arrived and started to work for the company, they got to know him better and discovered his other talents. Then in a serendipitous moment, they had unavoidable issues with the designer and plans for a show later in the season, and he was given the opportunity to take over.

Tom, at times, does a variety of jobs in the theatre, scene design, scenic art, technical direction, lighting design, and makeup. Being able to describe his work to people outside the industry can be difficult. It can even be challenging when he does scenic work, which is what he does most of the time, because the general public often doesn't understand the kind of collaboration and amount of different craftspeople that can be involved in one single production. They will often lump the work into one concept and ask things like, "Who built the set?" It always seems they are suggesting that one individual built the set and is solely responsible for its success. But Tom often likes to help educate these people by telling them that he was the scenic artist or the scene designer and give them a little information about all the other craftspeople and artists involved. He also likes to describe part of the collaboration that may have happened between the director and the creative team, so that they gain some understanding of this collaborative art. "Ultimately, I like to communicate that I am a part of a team that creates an environment that helps and supports the story," Tom adds.

PROFESSIONAL CAREER

When people walk out of the theatre they typically don't say, "Wow, the show was so good. Did you see that wood-grain paint treatment!" As the resident scenic designer and artist for Montana Shakespeare in the Parks (MSIP), Tom creates details that mostly go unnoticed. He paints and textures scenery, distresses doors

IMAGE 5.4 Annie *at the Ellen Theatre, Bozeman, Montana, 2017. Scenic design, charge artist, and technical direction by Tom Watson.*
Photo courtesy of Tom Watson.

and furniture to make them look old and lived in, and builds brick façades from plywood scraps. A lot of what Tom does on a daily basis is to take new construction and make it look like it has existed forever. Oftentimes he jokes that he has spent most of his career "painting wood to look like wood."

Tom's career spans three decades, working in various spaces. His work in outdoor theatres, traditional proscenium spaces, thrust theatres, black box theatres, and arena spaces has given him an overall appreciation to the craft. Tom has also built, designed, and painted scenery for trade shows, special events, and touring sets that need to break down small enough to fit in the back of pickup trucks. It seems like he learns something new every time he returns to each of the different venues. They all have their own advantages and disadvantages. Creating scenic elements for outdoor theatre, especially ones that also tour, have their own concerns often involving durability. Durability to withstand all the outdoor environmental issues is a common concern for his work. The pieces need to endure rain, sun, cold hail, mud, and wind. "You would think that wind might not be as much of an issue as some of these other elements, but sometimes wind can be the most destructive danger for scenic pieces," he states. Tom would often treat the outdoor items different than the same piece used inside. For example, set props such as a simple parlor palm in an urn that may create nice set dressing for a Noel Coward play would need to be significantly weighted down at the bottom for the outdoor set so it doesn't blow over in the wind. Tom discovered that solutions such as filling the base with plaster to secure the base of the plant into the urn works well. Materials in outdoor theatre scenarios also need to be considered. He often has to reinforce scenic art treatments more thoroughly with multiple layers of cheesecloth or using additional covering materials such as FoamCoat. As a nonprofit arts organization, part of the puzzle is keeping costs at a reasonable level. Even highly used adhesives such as hot glue (popularly used in the theatre) can be a disaster outside, as many types will melt in the hot summer sun.

As the resident scenic designer and artist for MSIP, Tom has always been loyal to the concept of collaborative art. "I love the theatre because it celebrates multiple artists working toward the same end game. In terms of scenic elements, I want to contribute what is needed, interesting, and significant to the overall storytelling dictated by conceptual direction that is communicated through the artistic leadership," says Tom. The director may typically drive this collaboration, but it can also be delegated to be more of a shared responsibility. Either way, Tom makes it a priority to understand the communal direction or take proactive steps to better understanding the primary ideas and vision.

The mission of MSIP is to make quality, live theatrical productions of Shakespeare and other classics accessible to communities in Montana and surrounding states with an emphasis on underserved, rural areas that would not otherwise have this opportunity. All performances are offered free, making Shakespeare in the Parks available to everyone. The company's oldest educational program, Shakespeare in the Schools, complements the education of young people by providing a complete production of one of Shakespeare's plays along with workshops that enhance their understanding and appreciation of Shakespeare's works. MSIP is known to bring in professional talent from across the nation. Hollywood star Bill Pullman, whose films include *Independence Day* and *Sleepless in Seattle*, started his acting and directing career with MSIP.

At this point in Tom's career, most of his work is now with MSIP, which is, in many ways, a nontraditional theatre company that does a lot their work outdoors. They are a traveling theatre company that travels nearly daily from one rural town to another performing in the local parks and other outdoor sights. They also travel with only an acting company and serve as their own technicians on the road.

One notable paint project that Tom shared is related to the work he has done with MSIP. He maintains a traveling stage that gets set up and torn down in city parks throughout the season. Often it is set up for one day and packed up after the show to be moved to the next city. It is designed out of stained and varnished wood that reflects an Old World Renaissance stage, and the nonpainted wood look works well in the natural sunlight and the summer green lushness of the city parks. Every summer it receives repairs, is restained, and gets a new coat of varnish. This treatment has been highly successful in preserving the cheap wood construction (pine and fir). It has kept the rain

IMAGE 5.5 *The Montana Shakespeare in the Parks summer tour stage gets a new deck and paint treatment. Production photo of* Othello, *2018. Evening performance in the Grove on Montana State University Campus.* Photo courtesy of Tom Watson.

and hail and occasionally snow (this is true, it sometimes snows in Montana in the summer) from accelerating damage from the elements. The only major issue was that the stage floor, treated in the same way, was often a danger for actors when the floor got wet from rain and the actors were trying to dance or execute fight choreography. It was a major problem. Tom tried some typical tricks in terms of grit in the finish but it still was a problem. The solution was to use flat latex paints and a water-based clear coating that matched the real wood look of the balcony, posts, and arches. This meant that the floor needed to be a scenic painted faux wood floor that also needed to live side by side with the real-world stained and varnished wood of the rest of the traveling stage. This all helped with the slippery floor issue while maintaining the original stained wood look that the audiences were familiar with.

PRODUCING THEATRE IN A FILM DEPARTMENT

"I view service to my allied arts field as an integral part of my role as an educator and artist, as well as a personal responsibility I have to contribute to the benefits of the learning environments I have come to appreciate over the years," Tom says. Montana State University eliminated the theatre program about twenty years ago, yet Tom is still able to produce theatre, teach production design and makeup, and serve the theatre community out of the department of film and photography. "Whether through university service or professional service to my field, I enjoy being a part of positive change and progress, and relish any opportunity to utilize my abilities to help advance the cause and mission of MSIP, as well as the theatre field as a whole. I take great pride in the projects and programs I have contributed to during my time in Montana," he adds. Some of the highlights of Tom's service have been in helping to define and direct the future of young theatre-makers.

As a theatre professional working in a film department, Tom has found ways to combine both his interests. Tom served as co-director of an Emmy-nominated documentary about a theatre company that he's spent twenty years of his life working with. *Bard in the Backcountry* is the story of Shakespeare in Montana. It's a behind-the-scenes look at a summer of MSIP—from first read through to final performance. For twelve weeks the actors work in an awe-inspiring landscape, getting to know rural populations who define rugged individualism. Communities statewide loves their Shakespeare in the Park, and this film highlights the way this love and landscape impact these young actors. "I started a documentary project about the company thirteen years ago and I am ready to finish what I started. It's an amazing company, and I have long wanted to tell this story and bring it to the people who love it like I do!"

Bard in the Backcountry chronicles a summer with the ten actors who make up this professional theatre company based in Bozeman, Montana, as they cover over sixty-five hundred miles to perform Shakespeare in the rural towns of this vast region. Along the way they encounter an array of characters, many of whom have been watching Shakespeare every summer for over forty years. We learn about the teamwork required to deliver a performance every evening in a new town and how the actors are also their own drivers, roadies, makeup artists, and set builders. *Bard in the Backcountry* reveals the mutual impact the tour has on the lives of these young actors and the people who put in the effort to bring Shakespeare to town. This journey provides a glimpse of the relevance that classic Shakespearean theatre still holds in the lives of everyday people across the region.

The film is a co-production of Cindy Stillwell's Hybrid Media LLC production company based in Bozeman, Montana, and MontanaPBS. Stillwell is the producer, co-director, and editor of the film. She and co-director, Tom Watson, both teach in the School of Film and Photography at Montana State University in Bozeman, as does the film's post-production supervisor, Theo Lipfert. The three professors were excited to collaborate on the film: "I love that my colleagues and I were able to work on this film together with

IMAGE 5.6 *MSIP stage sitting on Poker Jim Butte near Birney, Montana.* Bard in the Backcountry *had its world premiere screening at the Big Sky Doc Film Festival in Missoula, Montana, on February 8, 2015.* Photo courtesy of cinematographer Brandon Watson.

MontanaPBS. It was a real 'made in Montana' experience because the subject was Montana itself, really, with the homegrown Montana Shakespeare in the Parks having an amazing national reputation housed right next door to our film and photo school; then MontanaPBS, also headquartered in the same building as the film and photo school. It was a collaboration waiting to happen," says Stillwell.

"*Bard in the Backcountry* is a film I have been trying to make for over ten years. I knew this would be the right combination of people to make it a reality!" says Watson. "It really highlights some themes many of us relate to. The young actors are mostly new to Montana the summer they come out for the tour—and then, wow, what a tour they get! They go all over the state and we get to meet some of the long-time fans and characters that are faithful to this company. We meet these amazing characters through the eyes of the actors, who are outsiders, yet they are so cherished as they bring the words of the Bard to town," says Stillwell.

ARTIST BIO

Tom Watson is Associate Professor in the School of Film and Photography at Montana State University and the Resident Scenic Designer and Artist for Montana Shakespeare in the Parks. Originally from the Denver area, Tom received his BFA in Theatre at the University of Idaho and his MFA in Design and Theatre Technology from the University of Nebraska–Lincoln. He has also worked as an actor, director, scene designer, scenic artist, and lighting designer at various theatres across the country, including the Arrow Rock Lyceum Theatre, the Nebraska Repertory Theatre, the Idaho Repertory Theatre, the Snowy Ranch Summer Theatre, the Champlain Shakespeare Festival, the Country Dinner Playhouse, the Boulder Dinner Playhouse, the Montana Ballet Company, and Montana Theatre Works. Tom co-directed the documentary about MSIP, *Bard in the Backcountry*, which aired on PBS.

CHAPTER 6

DISTILLING AN ART, SHE CREATED A LEGACY

An Interview With Deborah Dryden

Erin Carignan

IMAGE 6.1 *Deborah Dryden.*
Headshot by Jenny Graham.

Deborah Dryden is an award-winning costume designer who has crossed boundaries between art, theatre, and technology to distill and describe techniques of painting and dyeing fabric. Although she is well known for her achievements as a costume designer, her book *Fabric Painting and Dyeing for the Theatre*[1] forever changed the field of costume design by contributing the first complete manual on the subject. It has inspired and informed generations of students and professionals to realize costume designs using textile mediums.

Dryden's study of textile painting and dyeing has produced a digestible manual for fellow and future theatrical artisans to use. This research further informed Dryden's costume designs while adding unique textures and colors to her costumes. She passionately believes that sharing knowledge spanning industries and academic departments is the key to inquiry-related theatrical artistry in costumes. She has a strong sense that the cross-pollination between different areas of study contributes to a richer foundation for all designers and artisans. Susan Tsu, renowned costume designer, colleague, and Dryden's contemporary, summarized her impact on regional theatre: "In thirty-seven seasons of the Oregon Shakespeare Festival [OSF]

Dryden's standard set the bar for all the other costume designers there. Her love of fabric painting and dying fueled the development and energy of the dye shop at OSF—and to this day, she continues to meet with the brilliant dyer/painters—women who have created magic in the [OSF] upstairs dye studio and whose passion carries on into their projects outside of the Festival."[2]

IMAGE 6.2 *Dryden's rendering for Lyubov in* The Cherry Orchard, *Oregon Shakespeare Festival, 2010.*
Photo courtesy of Deborah Dryden.

We sat down on a rainy Tuesday afternoon to chat over a cup of tea. The space was previously a one-bedroom cottage that has been converted to design and dye workrooms. The cottage is in a tree-lined neighborhood dotted with flowers against a backdrop of the evergreen-covered Siskiyou Mountains in Ashland, Oregon. The walls are lined with shelves full of books, a large cork board of inspiration images, a cutting table surrounded by vintage wood stamps, and many bins of dye and paint materials. Scattered throughout the studio are renderings of costume designers Dryden admires: Desmond Heeley, Lewis Brown, and some of Dryden's contemporaries, like Bob Morgan.

The upstairs workroom is a light-filled loft, accessed by a spiral staircase. This area houses her drafting board and art supplies for rendering, many more books, fabric swatches, and ephemera from her vast career. Dryden walked me through these processes, describing the back-and-forth process of moving costume pieces between the workroom and dye shop that results in the cohesive costumes that realize her designs.

Dryden's new studio was in the final stages of construction during my visit. It is a large garage space, behind her current studio, and features a roll-up window-filled firehouse door. It will have an eight-foot sink, a large cutting table, her library, painting and drawing materials, as well as a space for all her paint-dye materials. Here Dryden plans to continue her textile work and pursue her next endeavors post-retirement from OSF as the resident costume designer.

THE PENNY DROPS INTO THE SLOT: EARLY INFLUENCES

Dryden admits she wasn't interested in theatre as a kid. It wasn't until high school that she met and experienced work by costume designers who would change her path forever. She became fully aware of her love for costume design through family trips to the Stratford Festival in Ontario, Canada, and encounters with her father's colleagues in the theatre department of University of Wisconsin–

Madison (UW Madison) where her father was faculty of directing and playwriting. Although Dryden never felt pressured to work in theatre or academia, being in and around it during her formative years made a marked impression on her life's work as costume designer, academic, and painter-dyer. The first moment Dryden recalls wanting to be a costume designer occurred on a chance meeting during a high school career day.

DD: When I was in high school, a young recent Yale grad, a costume designer/ scenic designer, came to talk to my high school class about costume design. It was John Ezell, who is still a practicing scenic designer. He showed us his sketches for *Volpone*; I have very distinct memories of this. He is a beautiful artist and his costumes (he was designing costumes at that time) were all based on bird imagery, which is not unusual for *Volpone*, but I didn't know that at that time and I thought "Oh my god, this is so amazing!" And it was really one of those "the-penny-drops-into-the-slot" kind of moments . . . In high school, I had been interested in art, history, and theatre, and I hadn't found a way to make it coalesce. That really made me think "Oh, this would be a way to combine all those things that I'm interested in." So, I majored in theatre and John Ezell became my mentor and my teacher . . . He very generously allowed me to sit in grad design classes. I have to say it was pretty generous of the grad students, too, because you know they're paying to have special attention and here's this upstart in their midst! . . . I got a very huge education just by being around that level of other people's experience, [especially] to have John Ezell and Marna King as my teachers.

IMAGE 6.3 *Desmond Heeley's costume rendering for the character "An Actress,"* The Taming of the Shrew, *Stratford Festival Opera, 1973.*
Photo courtesy of Deborah Dryden.

Dryden's family spent many summers in Stratford, Ontario, the home of the Stratford Festival. This is where she was exposed to the work of several renowned designers and artisans, which greatly influenced Dryden's aesthetic as a designer.

DD: It was Desmond Heeley, Lewis Brown, Tanya Moiseiwitsch whose work I was watching [at the Stratford Festival]. I think very much I was influenced by all three of them. Particularly, I remained . . . influenced by Desmond's work [and] unfortunately

I only met him a few times. It wasn't like I had a really close connection with him unlike some of my colleagues. The vibrancy of both his drawing style and the way he made magic out of nuts and bolts, from hardware . . . at that time was new to me . . . I mean he was notorious, legendary . . . for taking, you know, a little bit of tissue paper and some hot glue and some bronzing powder and calling it armor!

EC: And it's gorgeous!

DD: It's gorgeous! So, his ability and Sam Kirkpatrick also, the ability to do that sort of theatre magic in the craft vein was very impactful to me. His use of color was very strong.

Inspiration from these artists can be seen in examples of Dryden's work. Many of her design choices feature texture, bold color, and magically pieced together garments from hardware and garden fabric that include dramatic transformations. In the example of *Macbeth* (OSF 2003), Dryden and the design team chose to create a stage that was a large pool of blood. Dryden's costume design featured the royal family in light hues, and throughout the play the characters become bloodier and bloodier. For this bold transformation, she chose fabrics that the blood could be washed out of every night, including a vinyl, polyester, and plastic breastplate pieced together with many common and inexpensive elements for Macduff. In another *Macbeth*, Dryden chose to create textures and patterns unique to each character. It is no wonder Dryden has been influenced by resourceful and imaginative designers who use heavy texture and pattern, often paired with bold color, in their designs, like Desmond Heeley and others.

IMAGE 6.4 *Dryden's intricate and washable breastplate created from hardware and other materials for MacDuff in* Macbeth, *Oregon Shakespeare Festival 2003.*
Photo courtesy of Deborah Dryden.

THE PATH TO A VIBRANT CAREER

During Dryden's undergraduate career at UW Madison she worked as a stitcher and other positions in summer stock. After graduation she worked as an assistant costume designer and teacher for a few years, then realized she wanted to pursue a higher degree. Dryden completed a MFA in Costume Design at UW Madison where she was immersed in gaining knowledge and techniques related to costume design and fabric painting and dyeing.

DD: It was a particularly vibrant time at the UW. Both politically (it was in the early 1970s) and artistically—there were some really phenomenal [faculty]. So [the environment] was fertile and the group of grad students were great—we all fed off each other.

EC: Did you get into your painting and dyeing during undergrad or grad school?

DD: Well, certainly intensively as a grad student because I was designing more shows . . . In school we all helped each other build our shows. We kind of did everything. If you designed it you were working on the show. We had no staff painter dyer so there was no one to do it.

After graduate school Dryden worked as a costume designer and painter/dyer in regional theatres. She talked about the early days of her career and the impetus for writing her book.

DD: I did work early on as a dyer painter intermittently. I did a couple shows at The [Old] Globe as a dyer-painter, this is many, many years ago. It was . . . the late 1970s with Bob [Morgan] on [*Midsummer Night's Dream*] . . . I was a substitute dyer painter at the Guthrie. That's where I first met Carrie Robbins. Their dyer-painter was off for a bit so I was like a substitute/interim . . . I worked briefly for another designer at OSF as dyer/painter, but have been primarily a designer here at OSF. For the most part, I don't consider myself really qualified to step into a full-time dyer painter position in the shop. Apart from doing that, writing the book, and my own interests, I feel like my work has primarily been as a costume designer. How does that manifest in terms of dye-paint? It doesn't always, as you know. I try not to force the design to go a certain way.

EC: But don't you think that having knowledge of dye and paint allows you to go further with your costumes?

DD: Absolutely, there's a real ignorance about what can and can't happen easily. When I was teaching I really tried to impress upon my grad students [to] really evaluate the situation you are going into. If they don't have a dye shop . . .

EC: You're the dyer!

DD: [*Laughs and nods.*] Or maybe this is part of how you design the show. Maybe this is *not* the show that you do 1,200 yards of dyed silk [*laughing*]!

When Dryden decided it was time to write a book on painting and dyeing for theatre, there were books by textile artists and scientists, but not one text organized to instruct and describe processes, materials, and tools used in theatrical dyeing and painting. Dyers worked on hearsay and with their own processes they developed. Textile artists were a separate discipline, and often their paths never crossed those of theatrical dyers. These artists had many published works, but dyers would have to own a whole library of books to mine all the information Dryden consolidated into one text.

EC: When you came up with the idea for your book, were you dyeing for your own designs or another designer at that point?

DD: My own [designs]. I think that was the impetus for writing the book in the first place, you know, that even now theatre can be a very insular world. It certainly was when I was in school and I didn't have any instruction about dyeing and painting and [was] frustrated and wanting to know more. Foolishly, I didn't even know enough . . . a year later I began to write the book [and realized] that there was a very vibrant textiles department on campus. No crossover. No connection between the two. But at the time I was flailing. In fact, I still have one of my graduate projects that was a dyed muslin screen printed thing. I heard a rumor that you could screen print with Rit dye and Tide . . . So I guess it sort of worked . . . it was a way to increase the consistency of the dye and it made it sort of like puff paint. So this was all hearsay . . . I figured, I really need to get some education! By the time I graduated, my first husband and I moved to San Diego to teach at UCSD [*University of California San Diego*]. Once I got there, I thought I really need to learn some stuff. So, I started contacting people who dye and paint fabric *not* in the theatre. I started taking every [dye and painting] workshop possible and I still do. It's been a savior for me and it's allowed me to learn so much . . . If I were to live this life again, I should've gotten a degree in textiles or an additional degree or something. I think some of my interest in workshops is trying to make up for the fact that I never went through a formal training program where people learn about dyes and paints and screen printing. So, I would say I'm self-taught, but that's not really true. I have learned from all these different workshop artists. And it's so much fun, I take at least one or two workshops a year now. The people I've been able to work with, even though it's short blocks of time, it just a huge learning experience for me. It's just been a wealth of information.

A few of Dryden's favorite workshops include Deconstructed Screen Printing from Kerr Grabowski and Carol Soderlund's workshop, Fiber Reactive Dye Chemistry. At the time of our interview she had just gotten back from the Alternative Marbling workshop with Elin Noble. When she was first exploring the world of textile dyeing and painting, she participated in a textile tour in Japan by Yoshiko Wada.

DD: That experience, plus the ongoing inspiration of Yoshiko's work in the shibori[3] world, has been hugely influential. That said, each textile artist with whom I have had the good fortune to learn from has been hugely influential in an indirect way in my design work.

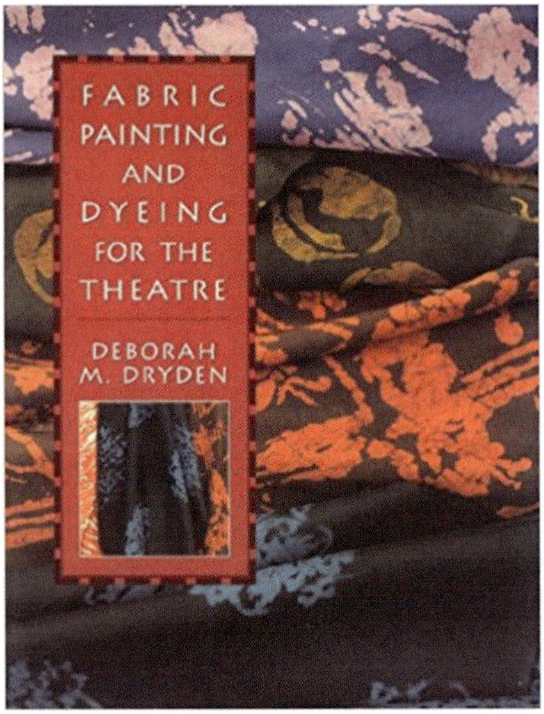

IMAGE 6.5 *Cover for Dryden's book* Fabric Painting and Dyeing for Theatre.
Photo courtesy of Deborah Dryden.

Dryden's interest in learning the processes of textile artists and applying it to her own art of costume design resulted in her book *Fabric Painting and Dyeing for the Theatre*. It is a straightforward compilation of processes and procedures related to painting and dyeing textiles, and it has been the go-to reference book for theatrical dyers, designers, and artisans for generations. It is a staple in every theatre artist's library and is a product of many years of workshops and collaborations with other textile and theatre artists.

Jack Taggart, an international A-list film painter dyer and breakdown artist, was one of Dryden's MFA students at UCSD. He comments on the importance of her book and the influence Dryden has had on his career: "Her master classes in dyeing and textile work were very enlightening. And of course, her book. It wasn't until I started getting work . . . on film and TV projects that I really got the chance to dig into the skills and knowledge I learned from Deb. All that stuff . . . suddenly rocketed me to the top of the field, years after the fact. I just feel like I try and do her proud by continuing her legacy on a global scale. I still make a habit of gifting her book to young dyers I've met through work, from LA, through Iceland the UK to Cape Town."[4]

A DEEPER LOOK: THE PROCESS OF EXPERIMENTATION

Dryden walked me through the costume design and textile production process of OSF's *Macbeth* (1996) and *The Tempest* (2007). Both are fantastic examples of her unique imagination and artistry in the complex layering of color and texture in the costumes of the royal family in *Macbeth* and in the Prospero robe from *The Tempest*.

In *Macbeth* Dryden decided she wanted to use real and false three-dimensional textures to represent the idea of a skewed reality present in the play. To find the textures, she took many photos of fabrics, costumes, trims, along with original textures and viewed the photos on proof sheets in the photo positive and negative. From these photos she chose which textures she wanted to use for creating photographic silk

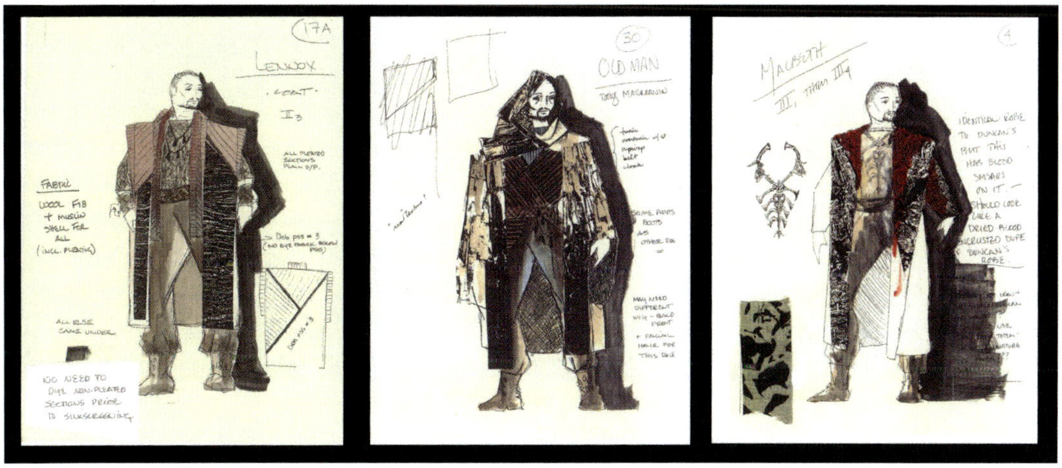

IMAGE 6.6 *Dryden's renderings using heavy texture for* Macbeth, *Oregon Shakespeare Festival, 1996.* Photo courtesy of Deborah Dryden.

screens. She then experimented with different textile media like fabric paint, thickened dye, and discharge paste.

DD: So, one of the things that I was interested in, in this particular production . . . was the idea in *Macbeth* of what you see isn't real, the idea of torqued reality, "What's fair is fair, what's foul is fair . . ." So, I thought it would be interesting, because it's outdoors . . . our largest stage, to play with two-dimensional texture, like the *illusion* of texture versus real texture . . . So, I started out by taking a bunch of photographs of textures of [items in costume] stock, some of them are just fabric. Then I . . . made larger images.

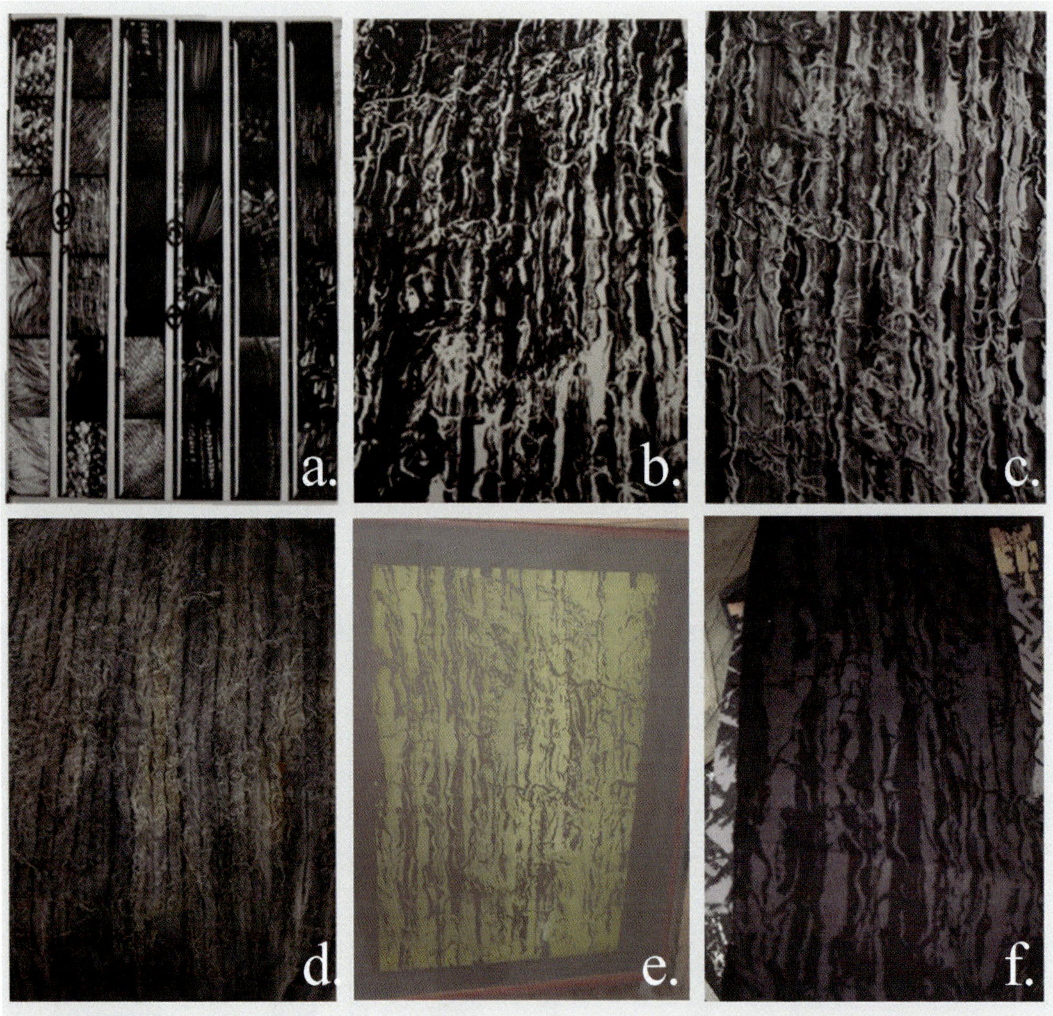

IMAGE 6.7 *(a) Photo negatives of textures for Dryden's* Macbeth *designs. (b) Detail of one negative in photo. (c) Photograph printed from negative in b. (d) Fabric used to create photo c and negative b. (e) Silk screen using photo negative b. (f) Fabric printed with silk screen in e.*
Photo courtesy of Deborah Dryden.

Dryden describes the textures and garments she used as sources for her silkscreen images.

DD: This is a texture of a fabric you can buy; this was some cheap-o velvet you probably recognize; this was a collar in stock with some smocking; and this one is [*she shows me the garment from stock*] this is a garment in stock that was many different colors before this, it's stripped since then. It was in stock so I took a picture of it, but it's, you know, it's just channel stitching multiple layers and just slicing through to the backing. Then you throw it in the washer and it gets all hairy . . . Well then I did sketches [*laughs*] . . . this was pre-digital age so I was doing shapes with Xerox sections to represent the textures.

EC: Are those Xeroxed from your texture photos?

DD: Yes. You know, cut and paste. When I did the sketches, I didn't have swatches. So, you can see the basic idea. It was a combination of what it could be real texture versus what could be flat, two-dimensional texture. So, the shop did a whole bunch of samples of real texture, real pleating, reverse pleating . . . and timed themselves, at my request . . . I ended up with a box of samples, and each one has an index card that said, "this is a pain in the ass and it takes about . . ." or "this takes 20 minutes." This is another one where it impacted the design, so something that was really somewhat labor intensive but rewarding, I could say "maybe this is a principle costume." Meanwhile, we were making photo silkscreens out of the chosen photos . . . We did a series of prototypes of just black and white [*she points from fabric sample to photo negative*].

EC: Look how great that looks in black and white and flat. It's totally different.

DD: So, it was a dyed muslin show . . . And then we . . . combined [real textures] . . . They were discharged [and] pleated, so you get the real texture against the visual. I could never, never, do that now . . . There's just not time anymore. I don't think we ever had copious amounts of time, but the idea of spending months doing R&D like this just doesn't exist anymore . . . Varying the texture of the base gives you a whole other dimension [*shows a piece of fabric silk screened then pleated*] . . . It was such a project and one that's fun to share because it's just such a puzzle . . . [It] just about killed everyone involved.

Dryden's imaginative exploration can also be seen in the spectacular Prospero's robe from

IMAGE 6.8 *Dryden's renderings using heavy texture for OSF's* Macbeth, *1995.*
Photo courtesy of Deborah Dryden.

IMAGE 6.9 *Derrik Lee Weeden as Prospero in* The Tempest*, Oregon Shakespeare Festival, 2007.* Photo by Jenny Graham.

an earlier production of *The Tempest* in 2007. Much like the production of *Macbeth*, this was a similar collaboration between the OSF costume workroom and dye shop.

DD: Prospero was being played by Derrik Lee Weeden on the outdoor stage. He's a very powerful actor and physical force. I thought it might be interesting to contrast his extreme masculinity with something that is more airy and feminine, kind of fighting against his force. And so that is why we went with sheers [*fabrics*]. I found an airline magazine with a picture of a talismanic shirt . . . they were mostly Arabic . . . [and] heavily inscribed with symbols. They were intended to protect the wearer from harm; they were considered magical garments. It was one of those "Oh my god, this is it [moments]!" We didn't want it to be specific to any religions' iconography, so the iconography was developed around multiple images that are shared by more than one religion, like certain symbols . . . [The outdoor stage uses sand to reduce slipperiness] for the actor, but it's like sandpaper . . . well that eliminates silk right off the get go. So we went to nylon organdy . . . [and] Chris Carpenter [*at the time head painter and dyer at OSF*] did a lot of these samples for me. We wanted the in-and-out color; we wanted the sense of parchment but not parchment . . . I chose . . . about four different shades, [not including] the [red] ombré part. And because there's one dyer painter, and there's the shop that's making the robe, I had to figure out a way to design it in such a way that it could be made in parts . . . parts could be painted in the dye room and [other] parts could be done in the workroom and assembled . . . I use this as a teaching example where the [technical] design actually informs the creation. I mean you have to—there's no way it could get done . . . It was really a puzzle!

DD: Then the ombré [*fabric is partially dyed a bold color that bleeds into another color or fades away completely, usually to the original fabric color*]. I had designed it ombréd, we were at dress rehearsal, and he wore it un-ombréd. The director loved it . . . it looked complete. And I went to the director and said "you know the ombré isn't on there yet, you think we should just say it's good?" Because it did look finished, I was really wavering, she said well "I like it, but if you want to do it . . ."
So, the next day I went to Chris

IMAGE 6.10 *(a) Layout of iconography on Prospero's robe. (b) Color swatches for Prospero's robe and the robe laid out for stamping.*

Photo courtesy of Deborah Dryden.

IMAGE 6.11 *Full Prospero robe with printed icons and red ombré dye.*

Photo courtesy of Deborah Dryden.

Carpenter and said "I'm scared, if we screw this up, it looks perfectly fine, we don't have to do it." And she said, "You designed it, we should do it!" So I said, "Ok, but I can't be in the room." And of course, she's a master at ombréing and she did it brilliantly and it was "Oh thank you that's what it needed." She saved me from my own self-doubt.

IN CONCLUSION

Dryden stands on the shoulders of several influential designers and textile artists who have used surface modification and texture in interesting and unique ways. From careful observation and participation in workshops and professional projects, she went on to formalize what she learned by compiling a book of methods and techniques that others could duplicate without all the individual R&D. This is a stunning accomplishment in the history of American theatre artistry, and her contributions continue to support generations of designers and artisans alike. On a personal note, this interview with Deborah Dryden helped me to plug into the foundation of theatrical design and artistry from which many of us have emerged. Dryden illuminated that sharing information with fellow theatre artists doesn't create compromise, it helps us live on in our art, while expanding our hearts and minds.

ARTIST BIO

Deborah Dryden has designed costumes for dozens of regional theatres, including ACT in San Francisco, the American Repertory Theatre, the La Jolla Playhouse, the Old Globe Theatre, the Seattle Repertory, the Alliance Theatre, the Alley Theatre, the Arena Stage, the Berkeley Repertory Theatre, the Denver Center Theatre Company, the Guthrie Theatre, the Huntington Theatre, Chicago Shakespeare, the Portland Center Stage, the Milwaukee Repertory Theatre, the Minnesota Opera Company, and the Mark Taper Forum in Los Angeles. She designed the costumes for the premiere production of Robert Schenkkan's *All The Way* for the American Repertory Theatre and on Broadway. Deborah considers the Oregon Shakespeare Festival to be her artistic home; she was the Resident Costume Designer from 1995–2014 and currently holds the title of Resident Costume Designer Emerita.

Dryden developed her interest in fabric painting and dyeing for the theatre throughout her career. Her work in that field resulted in the publication of *Fabric Painting and Dyeing for the Theatre*. She continues to explore new techniques in surface design and offers workshops in fabric painting and dyeing for the theatre at universities and theatres nationwide.

Deborah has received numerous awards for her work, including the national Michael Merritt Award for Excellence in Design and Collaboration and the USITT Distinguished Achievement Award in Costuming. In 2014 she received the Irene Sharaff Lifetime Achievement Award. Her designs have been exhibited at the Prague Quadrennial, the Bakhrushin Museum in Moscow, and the Lincoln Center for the Performing Arts. Deborah is Professor Emerita of Design at the University of California San Diego, where she taught costume design for seventeen years. She currently resides in Ashland, Oregon.

NOTES

1. Deborah Dryden, *Fabric Painting and Dying for the Theatre* (Portsmouth, NH: Heinemann Drama, 1993).
2. Susan Tsu, e-mail message to author, April 1, 2018.
3. Shibori is a Japanese technique of folding, tying, or knotting fabric before adding dye or paint. The folds prevent dye from absorbing into the fabric, creating a contrast in color.
4. Jack Taggart, Facebook private message to author, April 1, 2018.

CHAPTER 7

KEEPING AN OPEN MIND

An Interview With Daniel Weger

Jeannie Galioto

IMAGE 7.1 *Mr. Weger in his studio.*
Photo by Bethany Itterly.

Trying to find a time to talk with Daniel Weger is no easy task. He is a master tailor with multiple jobs and work days that are fifteen hours long. He is in demand, working with top celebrities on projects that everyone has heard of and seen, and yet he is not well known outside of the world of costume design. Weger admits, "Tailors are definitely behind the scenes."

Tailoring involves how to make a two-dimensional fabric fit smoothly around a three-dimensional person, and the term *tailor* has several definitions. To describe someone as a *master tailor* means they can create garments from scratch that will fit the intended body perfectly. This is no easy task considering how complicated the human body is with all of its rounded parts, bendable joints, asymmetry, and the fact that no two are exactly alike. Weger says he uses the title *patternmaker* because when he says tailor "people automatically think dry cleaner." He describes himself as somebody that "takes the human form and puts it on paper to make it into a garment."

Weger prides himself on being able to recreate period garments, and there are few

IMAGE 7.2 *Custom jacket for Tom Hiddleston as Hank Williams in* I Saw The Light.
Photo by Daniel Weger.

people who specifically pattern for men. He taught himself historical construction by taking vintage garments apart and putting them back together. This allowed him to see how the pattern pieces were shaped, and he learned about the specific construction details used in that era. "I think my work has focused almost exclusively on twentieth-century men's garments—and recreating them the way they were created the first time." His passion is the cut of the suit: the pattern and fit and having it look effortlessly sharp. Weger says his biggest reward is during the fitting process when his clients have the moment of "Wow! This looks really good!"

Weger grew up in North Carolina, the son of two Presbyterian ministers who encouraged his early interest in the arts. He describes himself as "a band nerd in high school" who played the trombone and trained as a classical pianist. "I really thought that was what I was going to do with my life." But, he continued to dabble in other areas of the arts. His mother advised he try theatre because it is a combination of all the arts. He attended Western Carolina University and pursued a theatre arts degree, acknowledging that "I acted my way through college very poorly." It was at this time that he discovered sewing as a work study assignment in his second year.

He then went on to receive his MFA in Costume Production from the University of North Carolina, Chapel Hill. During that time, Weger notes, "People would pull me aside and kind of condescendingly ask me, 'Oh what do you think you're going to make when you get out of here? Do you think you're going to actually have a job?' In fact, somewhere along the way, one of the Republicans in North Carolina singled out my grad school program as the most useless waste of taxpayer money and the education system. Obviously, there's the bias that working in the arts, you're going to be underpaid. I've found exactly the opposite."

During his undergraduate years, he attended the United States Institute for Theatre Technology and interviewed at the Santa Fe Opera booth on the showroom floor. They hired him as an entry-level stitcher, and David Burke, the costume shop manager, assigned him to the tailoring team. Weger says, "I started working with the tailor and just enjoyed it and worked with him for five years at Santa Fe through undergrad and grad school." This accidental summer assignment led to Weger's chosen career. Once he started tailoring, he got a couple of jobs and never looked back. "Ultimately you do your education, and much of what you do is through repetition and on-the-job work."

After Santa Fe, he moved on to the Shakespeare Theater in Washington, DC for a couple of years, and then went to a stitcher position at the National Opera. He was not quite ready to move to New York at that point; however, in 2011 he finally made that move. He first worked as the men's patternmaker for four years at Eric Winterling, Inc., a large costume studio that specializes in costume production for Broadway shows. From there he ventured out on his own with a studio in the Garment District in Manhattan for three years. It was difficult for him to afford the high rent and to keep people paid equitably for their advanced skill set. He did the fittings in-house, but his studio was smaller than most one-bedroom apartments. He created costumes for Broadway shows like *Of Mice and Men* with James Franco and some shows that were shorter, sixteen-week Broadway engagements. These productions would feature film and television actors wearing twentieth-century streetwear. He eventually transitioned out of theatre costume making because many current Broadway shows are large-scale Disney productions that need big costume shops to build gigantic costume numbers. He recalled at Winterling's "there was a team of sixty people that worked on one number for *Aladdin* for an entire month."

His first foray into film happened at a time when there weren't as many men involved in costume making, "I felt like a square peg when I started out." *Bram Stoker's Dracula*, designed by Eiko Ishioka, had come out, and Weger was inspired to believe "there is something in this for me and the dark creativity of that. The construction of that film made me aware that there was something other than ice show costumes and gorgeous dresses." He was, from then on, a huge fan of Eiko's film work and considers her one of his major inspirations. He jumped at the chance to work with her on *Mirror, Mirror*, her last film. His career came full circle with the opportunity to work with his idol. Weger recounts that "being able to make her acquaintance and do draping for her was a life goal of mine."

He credits much of his success to the tough love approach of both Judy Adamson at his MFA program as well as Eric Winterling. He studied how they interacted with different designers and learned how to communicate with them better. "I started out with the idea that the art of what I was doing, and the patterning, and being lost in what I was creating held me at one level for a while." He describes spending "a lot of time trying to over explain how to get from

FIGURE 7.3 *Custom jacket for Tom Cruise in* Mena. Photo by Daniel Weger.

point A to point B and it was something that—if people want a car, they know the car they want. They don't need to listen to the automaker explain exactly how the car is put together." Both Winterling and Adamson really stressed the value of communication to him. They both paid a lot of attention to the language the designer was using and would try to figure out a lot through what they are referencing. Weger remembers a costume fitting with costume designer Susan Hilferty that was problematic for him. Winterling pulled him aside to give advice: "This is what you need to pay attention to, you know you're paying attention to the pattern and what she is saying specifically. But what she has in mind is *Singin' in the Rain*." Weger says, "So coming up with pop culture references and the historical references and crossing over from a technical patternmaker to thinking with a design brain was valuable to me and helps me to this day." Weger realized he had to use a language with designers that doesn't have anything to do with the pattern or the techniques. It's all about the final product and the line of communication and the relationship that you build up as you work with the same designers.

He credits Eric Winterling with throwing him right into the flames. It was hard and demanding, but he was allowed to make his own mistakes and was pushed to produce. It was during this time that he developed his own method of drafting patterns. When he began working with Ben Stiller and Jim Parsons from *The Big Bang Theory*, he realized that once you start working at a certain level you are not able to get measurements from leading actors. He had to Google actors and assess their measurements from their photographs and make garments based on that. He began playing with old tailoring systems of human proportions, and he devised a way that if he could get an actor's height, weight, and chest measurement, then he could fill in the rest of the blanks. That basic information is typically available from the actor's publicist or from another wardrobe department. "The old tailoring systems have things like vest strap measures, and if you're looking at the old diagrams from the teens and 1920s, people are . . . [using] a tailor's square and a ruler and there's a seventy-year-old man holding a square up to somebody's back up from the floor . . . and that's just not the reality." He noted that if you are not taking the measurements yourself, you must have a lot of leniency. He has created a patterning system for both men and women, and would like to train more people to make patterns this way because it is particularly relevant to the entertainment industry.

FIGURE 7.4 *Custom suit for Method Man in* Deuce.
Photo by Daniel Weger.

His career has remained constant over the years due to his flexibility to work in television, music videos, ballet, bridal, alterations at various stores, film, theatre, and opera. He continually takes on side projects "When I was working in theatre, I'd take on film; if I was working in film, I take on theatre, and I do that to this day. It keeps things opened up for learning new experiences and trying to keep as dynamic as possible because the field changes a lot. I've not been without work for very long, but the film industry can dry up in an area overnight. I'm going to do essentially anything I can with a needle and thread to keep the lights on." He stressed the importance of keeping an open mind about the sort of projects that you take on and that there isn't any day job in the field that is beneath you. "People are wearing clothes their entire life and people will continue to get married and so there's something right there, even if it's not your first choice." While it may have seemed like taking a step back going from the Santa Fe Opera to David's Bridal, it turns out that he learned a lot of fast techniques that have helped along the way. That job taught him how much time things take and what kind of quality can be done in a certain amount of time, as well as time management. "I find that what I do has been relatively recession proof. Not to say I haven't had some severely hard times through it, but I've managed to own a home, support a family, and things like that. A lot of thinking on your toes, but you know it's a very resilient field. It's a field that once you're in with the community, then people definitely look out for each other."

When asked to choose his favorite venue to work in, he chooses film first since he gets more time to build pieces before production begins. "Television works at such a rapid pace that you sometimes have to leap in and say, 'What can we accomplish with the amount of time that we have?' It's more, 'This has been approved and now we have two days to do it, what are we going to do?'" He does regret, however, that film and television use so many actors and action that the intricate details of the costumes can go unnoticed. "Television especially is a lot of looking at one hundred fifty people that are in six seconds . . . total." He reminisces about a production of *Wozzeck* at the Santa Fe Opera that he worked on. "Wozzeck's perception of his wife became sluttier and sluttier as he became more jealous over her affair with the drum major. Her outfits were tighter, and her skirts were shorter. It was the same outfit, but in his perception, it was getting smaller and smaller. They can do things like that in operas and in theatre that they don't really do in film because it just looks like a continuity error."

FIGURE 7.5 *JJ Field in* Turn, *seasons 2 and 3.* Photo by Daniel Weger.

His current full-time affiliation is with a Marvel Studios Netflix series. He works with the designer Elizabeth Vestola and follows her from show to show; right now his main jobs are *Jessica Jones* and *Daredevil*. "That's the day job, and by 'day job' I mean up to fifteen hours a day Monday through Friday." He has a fully equipped shop at Marvel Studios. "I try to keep a scaled-down version so that I could literally in-house recreate any garment. That's a lot of what I do. If they need a leather jacket that looks just like this one . . . or there's always a sample of something." He has also done a lot of draping, especially on *Jessica Jones* because it has so many female characters. "It's a show that is directed by women. The top thirteen billed characters are all women in it and one man who plays a sidekick so it's a very female-centric show. For that reason, especially, I am happy to be involved and really proud to have been involved in that project."

IMAGE 7.6 *Custom jacket for Stephen Colbert.* Photo by Antonia Xereas.

Weger works with a long list of private clients, particularly celebrities such as Stephen Colbert and musician Jon Batiste. For Colbert, he did marathon fittings of fifteen or twenty suits at a time. He clarifies that he never made anything for Colbert from scratch, because for his whole run on *The Colbert Report*, Brooks Brothers would send him suits. Once you get to a certain level, the suit companies provide the suits in order to gain exposure. "The Stephen Colberts and the David Lettermans of the world don't pay for suits. They just get sent to them. Of course, I can't compete with that."

Weger has made around thirty suits for Jon Batiste over the past couple of years. "The fabrics are brocades and out-there kind of stuff. That's a contract that I've kept and not wanted to let go of, and really enjoy working with their team and the stylists for that show. It's a different kind of programming from what I normally do." To achieve the desired suit, Weger had many conversations with Batiste to get to the cut that he wanted. "It was clear in his mind that he had specific things that went back to his childhood of pictures. There was a suit that Prince wore and when I saw the picture it made a lot of sense. Pictures of a young James Brown in a very mod cut suit. There are elements of Michael Jackson, Prince, and James Brown that he made a mental picture of. Getting to that took a number of tries and back and forth and discussions to get to, but once we got to that, that's been his pattern that I've used for him. I've always been really happy to keep that up even though it does make for some sleepless nights."

At the time of this writing, he was working on an opera with a designer that he worked

IMAGE 7.7 *Musician and bandleader Jon Batiste in custom suit by Daniel Weger.*
Photo by Antonia Xereas.

with while at Eric Winterlings. "She was somebody that, even though it was a lower-paying position, I wanted to work with her, so I did and will continue to do things like that. There will be designers that I've worked with in the past and sometimes I do work at a loss for them. They bring me on to bigger projects when they get them. You can't be the person that says no repeatedly because eventually you will be the person that nobody calls."

For Weger, the biggest challenge has always been time. There are lots of overnight shifts and spending lots of money to get supplies quickly, but he still finds his career very rewarding. He enjoys the artistic output. "This is going to sound really cliché and hokey, but the work that I'm doing is going to be there long after I'm gone. You know millions of people have seen the work that I've done, and that's something that I find very enjoyable and very rewarding. I never wanted to be very visible about my work, but I still get satisfaction knowing it's there and I've done it and my kids, or grandkids, or people who knew me can look that up and see something years from now."

ARTIST BIO

Daniel Weger is a patternmaker and tailor of men's and women's garments with well over a decade of custom tailoring experience. Beginning as a costume assistant in college, he later worked his way up from the alterations floor in a dry cleaners to patterning suits for film and television. His experience in-between ranges from Broadway to commercial and retail suiting, opera, theatre, fashion, and bridal. He holds an MFA in Costume Production from the University of North Carolina at Chapel Hill, with a focus in classically tailored men's garments, post–Industrial Revolution, c. 1750–1950. His regional theatrical work includes the Santa Fe Opera, the Washington National Opera, and the Shakespeare Theatre Company. He has been the head tailor at New York studio Eric Winterling, Inc.

Recent film and television work includes Marvel's *Jessica Jones, American Gods, Quantico,* HBO's *The Deuce,* AMC's *Turn* (seasons 3 and 4), *The Bleeder, The Late Show with Stephen Colbert,* Fox's *Gotham, Steve Jobs,* and *I Saw The Light.* Broadway credits include *Finding Neverland, Of Mice and Men, All The Way, The Nance, Annie, The Book of Mormon, The Heiress, War Horse, Phantom of the Opera, Harvey,* and many others. He has patterned and sewn garments for many top actors, including James Franco, Michael Fassbender, Tom Cruise, Tom Hiddleston, Bryan Cranston, Kelsey Grammer, Jeff Daniels, Philip Seymour Hoffman, Nathan Lane, Ben Stiller, Dan Stevens (*Downton Abbey*), David Strathairn, Jim Parsons (*The Big Bang Theory*), Forest Whitaker, and many others.

Originally a North Carolina native, Daniel has made New York his home to carry on the wonderful tradition of classically tailored menswear. A practitioner of a dying art form, he strives to provide suitings with the same techniques used by master craftsmen over a century ago.

CHAPTER 8

PROP MASTER JAY DUCKWORTH

A Star Among Us

Jessica Hansen

IMAGE 8.1 *The artist at his studio.*
Photo by Monica Simoes. *Courtesy* of Jay Duckworth.

Jay Duckworth is a Renaissance man, a polymath. He is an explorer, artist, historian, psychologist, creator, innovator, astronomer, scientist, magician, master craftsman, philanthropist, educator, and mentor. Most importantly, he is infectiously generous. Duckworth believes that you must share your knowledge and skills to touch people's lives, to stay alive well after you are dead. He explains that there are visionaries and revolutionaries. "A visionary can envision a better world using their creativity, skills, and wisdom. A revolutionary sees that same vision, acts upon it, makes it a reality and continues to explore with infinite curiosity." Jay Duckworth is a revolutionary. He is creating a legacy as an artist and craftsman and is trying to create a theatre world of equality, focused on the art and serving the story. His generous spirit has fueled his lifelong endeavor in education. It sounds pretty epic and ambitious for someone who calls himself a "proptologist," but Jay's unique sense of humor is yet another gift he shares. He even resembles a Renaissance man, with strikingly similar features to Henry VIII, period muttonchops, and a full history to match from within the historical archives of his brain.

Speaking to Duckworth is like opening an endless book full of philosophical anecdotes, fantastical theatre lore, detailed technical drawings, scientific recipes, inspirational quotes, and historical information. He says, "Everything that you ever want is just on the other side of fear. It's a total illusion holding you back." With Jay, the only "illusions" exist when he creates magic on stage with props. His knowledge, story, experiences, skills, and generosity are an open book. His bravery, daring nature, and ability to think and act outside the box encourage those working with him to rise up. "See the future that you envision, [work] on it and make it a reality." He is starting a revolution and wants you to join him.

AN EXPLORER

It takes the spirit and bravery of an explorer to discover what it is that excites them in the world. For Jay, this process will never end because every new experience and skill excites him. Growing up in Missouri, he did not know that he wanted to be a props person, but he did recognize the moments that made him feel alive. Duckworth describes, "When you tip too far back in a chair, where you are like 'I am going to die,' then you are truly alive. Every part of you is electrified." These pivotal moments served as a map, guiding his creative artistic career in allied crafts when all other paths could have led him to be a more conventional designer.

When Jay was a young kid most people would have described him as a precocious child, but he describes his younger self as a pain in the ass! At one time, after getting lost, he promised himself that he would never go through that again. He decided that he needed to learn the necessary resources to survive in the world on his own. He started to study the stars. His love for astronomy led him to a celestial exploration of constellations. Duckworth was intrigued and began to wonder why the constellations have Greek names but the stars have Arabic names. It just didn't make sense, so he continued to read, study, question, and explore. He immersed himself in ancient wisdom and mathematics with a mission to go back to the basics to be informed. His craft was born. Now when Jay is working he never gets lost. He always goes back to the history, back to the basics, and back to the "why." This knowledge is not just for his personal state. In his truly generous and selfless nature, he wants to be the "go to person" in the room because it fills everyone with confidence. It raises them up.

From the start, Jay Duckworth had the makings of a props person in his blood. His mother was an artist and his father worked construction and they both shared a love for history. When he was seven years old he visited the *Dracula* set at Universal Studios with his parents. When he saw them demonstrating the chocolate syrup used for stage blood he turned to his mom and said, "THIS is what I want to do!" This electrifying moment was another discovery leading him on his journey, and it became his focus. At the time in a small town in Missouri, his mom thought that what he wanted to do was act, and so they sent him to acting classes. His parents were incredibly encouraging, and Jay continued to study theatre through high school, but the day after graduation began a whole new journey!

Duckworth began his professional career the day after high school graduation. After all, when you are becoming a Renaissance man, there is no time to waste! He started summer stock at the Mule Barn Theatre in Tarkio, Missouri. He was hired because he could work in the carpentry shop, act in some shows, and he knew how to play the bagpipes, which saved them from finding someone to play in *Brigadoon*. Jay says that this kind of apprenticeship hands-on experience is the best experience that you can have because each show has a challenge and opportunity to learn. He says, "That could be why I push myself so hard because you learn so quickly in order to get as far as you can in summer stock. You need a mentor though, you need someone to work with, and someone above you to show you the short cuts." That mentor was Allen Cutler, an ex-Benedictine-monk props master from the George Street Playhouse in New Jersey. He took Jay under his wing and saw his potential in props. It wasn't until their paths crossed that Jay really noticed props as an art form or craft, until then, they just sort of appeared. Cutler told him, "Let's teach you what you are talented at," and taught him that every prop has a purpose and a reason for being. This type of generous mentoring continues to inspire Jay to share his knowledge with others and take them on his journey. Cutler helped him explore his talent to its full potential. "I could have kept building different sized boxes for the rest of my life without his guidance. I really enjoyed props because I could put my mark on a production. I saw the difference a good props master can make on not only the show but to round out an actor's performance as well," Jay states.

After moving from Missouri to New York, it took Jay eleven years of brave exploring to get his first Off Broadway show. On his journey, he has worked in every kind of theatre: outdoor, in the round, proscenium, thrust, black box, profile, community, melodrama, LORT, Off-Off Broadway, Off Broadway. In that time he developed a mantra, "My work is my name and reputation." And his work and his reputation are exactly what landed him his dream job as the resident props master at The Public Theater in New York City. As a child, their production of *The Pirates of Penzance* gave Jay that feeling of leaning back in your chair and being truly alive. He gets to live that feeling every day, but an explorer does not just stumble upon riches. Jay Duckworth studied the stars and created the path that led to his dream.

A MASTER CRAFTSMAN

An apprentice studies for years before becoming a journeyman and continues to practice before becoming a master craftsman and Renaissance man. Duckworth has had decades of fascinating theatrical experiences with fascinating theatrical legends, or as he calls them "Theatre Royalty." After all, he is akin to Henry VIII and his court is a group of revolutionaries trying to change the face of the creative and collaborative theatre process. Jay approaches the creative and collaborative process with the basics in mind. He explains, "First there was the WORD. It is like the Bible."

He immerses himself in the text and tries to envision the world and the story it tells. Then he highlights all the physical props in yellow, environment and blue, perishable props in red, and incidentals in pink. He explains that an incidental could be a "prostume," or prop-costume. Once you know the story and the world, the real magic begins.

If Jay asks you to tell a joke, he is not just looking for a good laugh. He says that he knows that he has "made it," because he has had a Cue-to-Cue (Q2Q) comic written about him! Jay can predict the creative process with someone new by asking the person to tell him a joke, and if they can tell a joke then he knows that they will have a good creative process. Why? Because they understand how to tell a

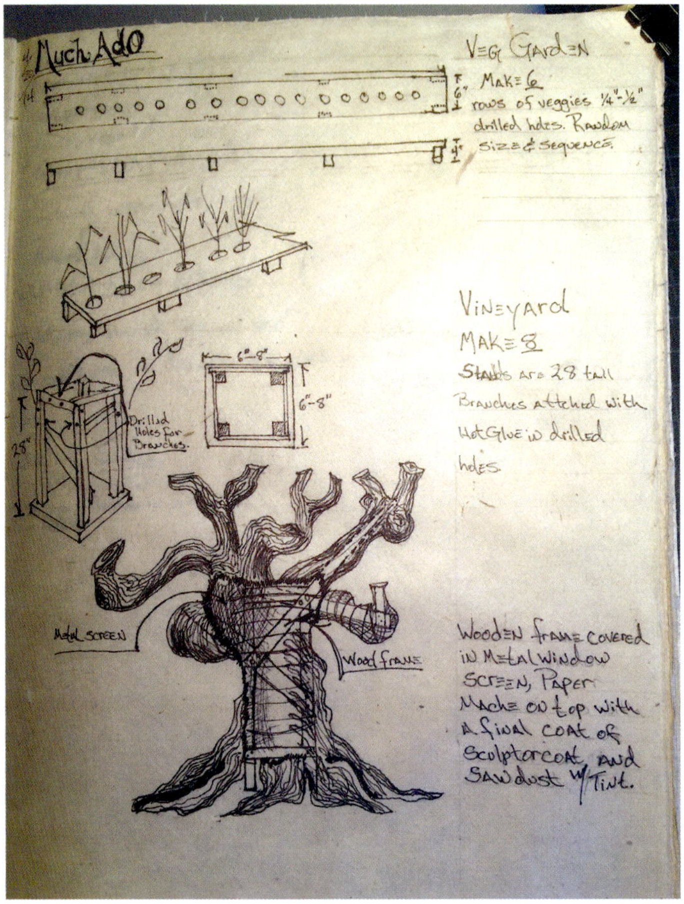

IMAGE 8.2 *"Always do hand-drawings to keep your skills up and to help others visualize the structure, as well as the art, of the end-product."*
Courtesy of Jay Duckworth.

story with a beginning, middle, and end. If not, then he has to prepare for a disjointed creative process without an arch.

The props master can be a tough position because the props master has to please a production manager, director, designer, and actors. Jay shares that it goes back to the basic skill of listening; listening to how people talk and the words that they use. If they describe feelings, then they are tactile, and you should provide them with something to touch. If they describe something they are seeing, then they are visual and communicate through images and pictures. His advice is, "If you want someone to make a decision, you give them one thing that is absolutely not right, one that is correct and affordable, and one that is perfect and too expensive. It gives the person the illusion of choice, which I learned from magic. It is like Hobson's choice. It's a choice that subconsciously you don't know you are forced into making and you feel better by making it." Jay believes you need to be actively listening and try to conform to someone else's comfort zone, proving that he is part psychologist and magician in the collaborative process.

IMAGE 8.3 *Comic strip featuring Jay Duckworth.*
Image provided by Q2Q Comics by Steve Younkins.

Jay Duckworth's mastery in props developed by working with "Theatre Royalty." He has endless anecdotal tales full of theatre lore and legendary names. Jay made a steak for John Lithgow out of watermelon, and when he demonstrated cutting the "steak" Lithgow replied, "I hope my performance is as good as this steak." He created a guillotine for a Terrence McNally production, which had to work correctly, every single night . . . or else! Jay said he had no idea how to create that consistency but cockily told everyone that they sure were lucky to have him working on that then. And it did work, every single show. Jay has worked with the likes of Steven Sondheim, Christopher Durang, and Terrence McNally. He says these "career starting" legends treating him as an equal is one of his greatest honors. Among them, "you realize this is a different world where everyone is equal. There is no one bigger than anyone else. You are in Oz," says Jay.

In his tenure at The Public Theater as the props master, Jay has created props for a huge variety of theatre genres, from Shakespeare to Brecht, from musicals to new original work, from Greek to contemporary. Jay says, "We make our own luck. If opportunity is not knocking, kick a hole in the wall and make a door." When there was an opening at The Public Theater for a props master, Jay kicked a hole in the wall, made a door, and added a medieval drawbridge to protect his opportunity! He collected seventeen letters of recommendation from the "Theatre Royalty" in his career. He arrived at the interview with those letters and a finely branded portfolio and said, "I understand that this interview is a formality. You all come very highly recommended." They laughed and complimented him on his sense of humor. He was not going to let this opportunity pass him by because he felt a strong connection to the values and philosophy of The Public Theater. Just like Joe Papp, the theatre's founder, Jay dreamed of making theatre for the people to help democratize art. Jay joined that revolution and is sharing its message through each prop on stage and by working with fellow artists as equals who share and uplift one another. This has become Jay's version of "Oz." It should be mentioned that Jay Duckworth won't rest on his laurels. Despite all the exploring and mastery that he has achieved in his career, he still believes

IMAGE 8.4 *Duckworth working on a prop for* Cymbeline *at Shakespeare in the Park, July 24, 2015.* Photo by Bob Cooley. *Courtesy* of Jay Duckworth.

that you need to keep practicing. If you would like to get better at anything, then it shouldn't always be easy. He says, "Thank god it doesn't because we are always getting better. There is a cellist in his late eighties that practices every day and someone asked him, 'Why are you still practicing? You are a master.' He replies, 'I think I am getting better.' When you are walking around, you are not living your life. When you are really honest to god living your life, you are living 20% out of your comfort zone." This is what makes him a polymath, with an infinite desire to learn more, share more, and do more.

A HISTORIAN

It is no coincidence that the stars aligned and brought Jay Duckworth and Lin-Manuel Miranda's award-winning *Hamilton, An American Musical* together. Jay's ferocity for history and knowledge have set an extremely high benchmark in the industry, with an attention to detail that borders on the psychotic. He brings in as much history as he can about an object because it needs to carry weight and have history and interest in order to serve the basic story. As an example, he once taught himself to drop spin wool for a production of *As You Like It* in order to teach the actress playing Rosalind.

He also explored different early writing styles from the Iron Age on leather scrap, and he sewed tree bark and dried clay block for *King Lear*. He is able to focus on the research, the work, and the execution, thanks to his staff at The Public Theater. His approach is to create props as museum pieces that are

IMAGE 8.5 *Duckworth produces his own wool; he cleans it, cards it, and spins it. He starts with single and works up to plied yarn. He likes to leave the bottom open and undone to show potential mentees how the weave is made.*
Courtesy of Jay Duckworth.

beautiful, accessible, and draw people into the environment emotionally. He is able to "gild the lily."

Jay Duckworth asked Ron Chernow, author of *Alexander Hamilton*, the book that inspired the musical, to be as critical as possible about the historical accuracy of the props as they sat in the theatre to watch the first preview. In the true fashion of a master craftsman, explorer, and historian, the props in *Hamilton* were practically pulled from the Founding Fathers themselves.

For the handwritten paper props, Jay used a program called LetterPerfect, which captured each letter of the alphabet in the original hand of Hamilton, creating an authentic font.

The newspapers were recreated from an original publication's articles and the map used on stage is actually a reproduction of Rochambeau's map. It is a history buff's dream

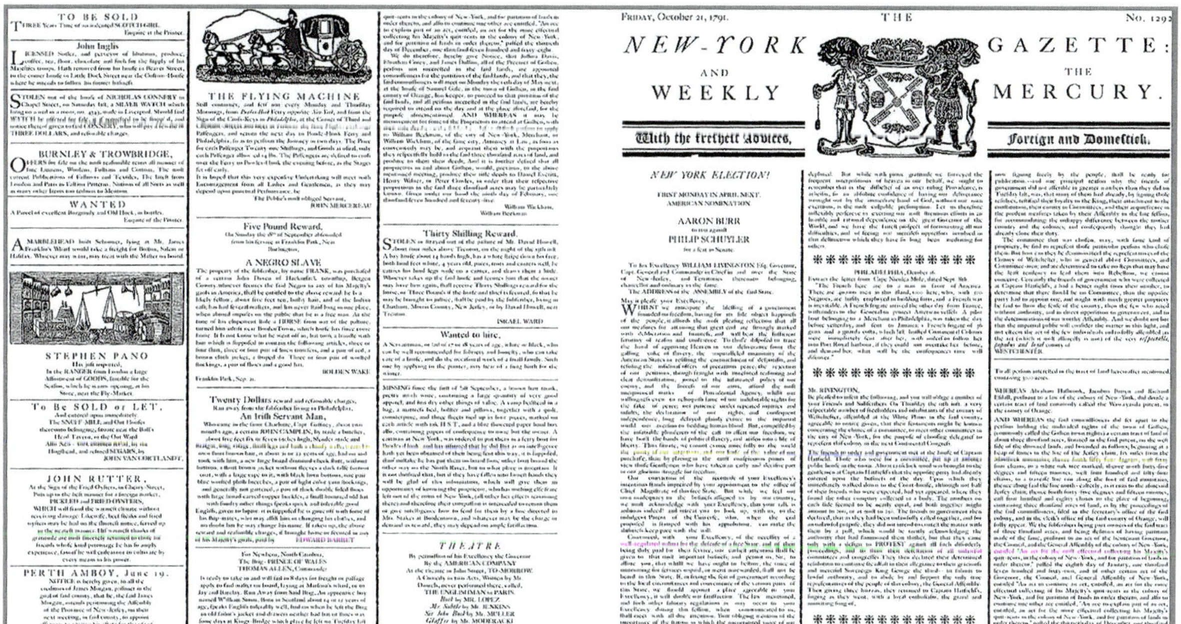

Friday, October 21, 1791. THE No. 1292

NEW-YORK GAZETTE: AND THE WEEKLY MERCURY.

With the freshest Advices, Foreign and Domestick.

IMAGE 8.6 *The newspapers featured in the musical* Hamilton *were recreated from an original publication's articles.*
Courtesy of Jay Duckworth.

AUDIO COSTUMES LIGHTING PROPS SCENERY THE PUBLIC. PRODUCTION DEPT.

HAMILTON

Prop Bible

Hamilton Act 2 Desk

Vendors	**Legs:** Adams Wood Products – Claw & Ball with Carved Knee – Soft Maple – Part# ACBCK29-1 – 29 ¼" x 1 ¾" Desk Leg **Applique:** Decorators Supply – Shell w/ Ribbons &Leaves – Part #5767 – 5 1/8" x 14 ¾"
Dimensions	60" x 28" x 30"
Paint	• Base: Blend of Red Mahogny Minwax 225 & Special Walnut Minwax 224 • Sealer: Benjamin Moore, Stays Clear Low Luster • Painted a blotter onto the desk with a blend of acrylics • Added a decorative gold trim around the edge of the "blotter" with a gold paint pen
Build Notes	• Drawing from DKD • Added a false bottom to hide guts of set screws & construction of table • Set screws inserted into the table top so that 3 props could be attached with wing nuts and stay in place when the table is picked up in the air
Preset Location	Onstage from We Know
Additional Notes	Everything but Ledger is attached to the desk

sswanberg/svance 2.39 Hurricane 4/22/15

IMAGE 8.7 Hamilton, *Act 2 desk specs.*

Courtesy of Jay Duckworth.

come true. Chernow asked Jay why he was doing all this, and he replied that everyone else had lifted themselves up and set the bar so high. They knew that together they were changing the face of musical theatre since the first read through. Duckworth says, "It is an incredible feeling to know that you were changing history. This was our *Showboat*. There was nothing like *Showboat* before *Showboat*. There was nothing like *Oklahoma* before *Oklahoma*." The next day, Jay went to the filming for the 2016 Grammy Awards where *Hamilton* won for Best Musical Theater Album.

Jay studies history for himself, for his art, and for his shows, but he also studies history to share it. He surrounds himself with books and marks them for reference. He writes his own books and records recipes, tips, thumbnail drawings, and yearly goals. He evaluates each year, sets goals, and assesses his values. At the end of each year, he re-evaluates. You can find almost all the answers about the world out there in a book, but sometimes people are the ones with the answers. Jay says, "Art is the only things that teaches you about yourself. You have to be able to go out and listen to people. From those people you get the most and you have to surround yourself with people that are smarter than you and more skilled than you so that you are always growing." Jay's quest for knowledge is infectious and his generosity to share it is a true gift for those who are ready to accept it.

A CREATOR, MAGICIAN, AND INNOVATOR

Those who are always reaching for the stars develop tips, tricks, secrets, and solutions that can only be learned through hands-on experiences. Jay Duckworth continuously strives to try new technologies, experiment with different materials, and share his trials and tribulations of "propdom" with his peers. All props masters share the same love for balancing problem-solving and a keen sense of the philosophy of aesthetics. He insists that the work he does is absolutely seamless, and that if it is done right no one should see it at all.

During his career Jay has seen many changes and developments in the industry, including advances in technology, safety improvements, and in the way show business works. Speed is a huge factor now due to the increased use of computer software and digital information, changing the process of his work. Jay explores new techniques by watching YouTube tutorials and saves inspiration sources on Pinterest, a Web-sharing platform. After all, how else do you learn to make Viking horns from paper towel rolls? He incorporates 3D printing, Photoshop, and casting into his work, taking his final products to the next level. He uses unique materials to problem-solve.

For example, how do you create high-gloss cube furniture that weighs less than two pounds and can handle the weight of an actor? Duckworth's answer is a combination of gator board, foam, and self-leveling fiberglass, plus a little R&D mixed in—and all of this within budget. He believes that when artists have endless resources they have no place to be creative, and, in turn, to be inspired by someone else's creation. He mixes technology with conventional methods and materials in his work to cross-pollinate and innovate.

Duckworth gets work as a props designer both from word of mouth and from his website. He says, "Once you get your first two jobs in props, because there are so few good props people out there, work will find you. We have so many facets of skills. I could go out there

IMAGE 8.8 *Fire-red Mylar used at the end of logs with blackened sea glass and controlled light. It goes from "hot to cold" on stage.*
Courtesy of Jay Duckworth.

and freelance as a carpenter, electrician, pattern cutter, stitcher, etc. Once you establish your name and do really well, your names catches on quick because it is such a small community." At this point in his career Jay Duckworth is constantly working because he has made a name for himself. He does attract work from his website and attributes it to the rave reviews and recommendations that he receives from those who work with him. His generosity spreads so wide that his portfolio, both in print and online, is not only a representation of his work but also an archive of tips and how-to strategies for fellow props people. While he believes that he is a creator, magician, and innovator in the prop world, Duckworth still feels that he has much to learn. He would like to continue working with casting and molds, as well as with teams that create haunted houses. He is fascinated by the tenacity and creativity of the cosplay community, and admires their innovations with varied skill levels and low budgets and says, "You are learning stuff from people that have a different approach seen through new eyes." There are so many things on Jay's list that he insists on writing them in a Google document, because there are just too many to mention!

A PHILANTHROPIST

As a member of a community, Jay believes that everyone should contribute in the way of community service. This in-kind service is selfless, nourishing, and for the love of the craft. He thinks that if there is one thing that he has contributed to his community, it is a sense of unity. Jay's community service is how he spends his rare day off and his vacation time. In order to survive in such a competitive industry, many artists have developed a thick skin and a defensive attitude toward sharing information. Jay calls this "The Cult" and has been fighting against it with a revolutionary approach to change the culture through positivity and openness since 2009. Duckworth doesn't want anyone thinking that he is some "really sweet" guy though. He admits, "I talk a good game, but I am very egotistical and I push myself hard because I am very ambitious. I am ambitious but I think we should all help each other out." This is why he created the Prop Summit, a yearly meeting of Broadway, Off Broadway, LORT, academic professionals, and students in New York City. It began as a thank you to all the people who helped him through his first year at The Public Theater, where they discussed working techniques, resources, and networking. Now everyone is welcome, and it is an annual summit. It has featured sessions with fight choreographers, weapons experts, representatives from Rosco, 3D printing experts, food safety lectures, the head of the Broadway Green Alliance, and the executive director of Materials for the Arts. "We don't own anything truly until we can give it away. Don't serve yourself, serve the art, period," he says. It is the insecurity of artists that make them hold on to their ideas, making them weaker. Jay created the Summit as a way to spread his word that we should raise each other up and that we only become better when we share information, and his revolution is catching on.

Jay's community service extends to the incredibly lucky interns who study with him at The Public Theater during the summer. When they start they receive a moleskin notebook, and inside they write:

1. Be honest.
2. Be helpful.
3. Be true.

It is very simple; it is going back to basics. It is finding your place in the world by using the stars as a guide. While the interns study with him, they research the Stone Age until the Industrial Revolution for three months, giving presentations on important historical figures; learning where things come from, and their particular use and meaning in historical times; and how to build their own props. Duckworth explains, "This is the kind of stuff that I live for! I can impart this information to young people. I tell all my interns that this will change your life. You will not see anything the same way from this point out. That is a warning. If you don't want to change, don't come into this place. It will be hard, and it will be intense." He is hard on them because they are "hand-picked" talent from around the United States, and he pushes them to reach their potential, just like Allen Cutler pushed him as a young man at the George Street Playhouse.

Being recognized by educators and invited to share his wealth of knowledge with students are Jay's proudest moments. The students are the future of theatre, and being invited to a place where he can touch the next generation of artists is a distinct honor. Jay Duckworth is an active participant in the Kennedy Center American College Theater Festival (KCACTF) and has served as a keynote speaker. One of his favorite moments was meeting and talking with a young man at the front desk of The Public Theater, who said Jay was much like the amazing person who was the keynote speaker in KCACTF Region 7 about three years ago, and that the keynote speaker was the entire reason that he had moved to New York. Jay asked him, "Was it about ripping up a dead body? Because I am THAT guy!" It is no surprise that Jay's generous spirit is guiding him toward working with the future artists in theatre and may perhaps find him in academia one day.

IMAGE 8.9 *Skull by Jay Duckworth.*
Courtesy of Jay Duckworth.

JOIN THE REVOLUTION

If you aren't inspired yet, then it is time to tip back in your chair too far until you feel electrified and truly alive! All of us—designers, technicians, artists, directors, stage managers, and theatre practitioners—need to take a page from Jay Duckworth's book and elevate ourselves from visionaries to revolutionaries. The world of props can unify all the passions of a polymath, from history to astronomy, science to magic, ancient techniques to cosplay. There are no rules and there are no limits to your imagination, just illusions holding you back. So get an empty notebook, be honest, be helpful, and be true. Explore the world both past and present with curiosity and create magical innovations that you will share with generosity. Rise up!

IMAGE 8.10 *Duckworth's proptologist logo.*
Courtesy of Jay Duckworth.

ARTIST BIO

Jay Duckworth is the founder of the Prop Summit, a yearly meeting of Broadway, Off Broadway, LORT, academic professionals, and students every autumn in New York City. He has been the keynote speaker for the Kennedy Center American College Theater Festival (KCACTF) and a guest of the United States Institute for Theatre Technology (USITT) numerous times. He was the first props master to be invited to work with the Stagecraft Institute of Las Vegas (SILV). He has lad master classes in properties at several universities. His portfolio includes original work for starts in remastered classic Greek theatre, reimagined Shakespeare plays, musicals such as *Hamilton*, as well as stark Brechtian shows. His tenure continues at The Public Theater in New York City with contemporary and ink-wet works. Jay has made it his mission to push the discipline of props to be the highest art that it can be. His knowledge of history, science, and the arts is breathtakingly broad and profound, and his practice of ancient crafts is admirable. Passing that information and passion for excellence on to the next generation is paramount to him. He boasts over thirty years of experience in LORT and Off Broadway theatre, fast-paced summer stocks, independent films, TV, and music videos.

Samples of Jay Duckworth's work can be seen at his main website www.proptologist.com, the NYC Props Summit www.nycpropsummit.com, plus Erik Hart's Prop Agenda www.props.eric-hart.com and *The Prop Building Guidebook*: www.propbuildingguidebook.com

CHAPTER 9

THE NONTRADITIONAL JOURNEY

An Interview With Samuel Lee

Leah Ramillano

IMAGE 9.1 *Samuel Lee.*
Photo courtesy of Samuel Lee.

Samuel Lee is the crafty and innovative mind behind Prince Armory, a company based in Houston, Texas, dedicated to creating personally customized and wearable leather armor. He creates pieces for private clients who are passionate about cosplay culture as well as commercial clients within live performance, events, and advertisement. His nontraditional journey to success can be attributed to his father's artistic craftsmanship, Renaissance Festivals, and the online artistic community of DeviantArt. I spoke with Lee about his process and how he came to develop the strikingly ornate work that Prince Armory produces.

"I grew up in a small town in Texas—nothing too interesting to talk about here—but my dad was a jack-of-all-trades, so I was exposed to fixing and creating things. That probably helped shape my path in life." The way his father bridged the gaps between practicality, skill, and art helped influence Lee's fascination with creative tinkering.

IMAGE 9.2 *Leather armor inspired by the film* Wonder Woman.
Photo courtesy of Samuel Lee.

His father was employed by the government as a maintenance supervisor at a prison system, where he was responsible for the repairs and the overall upkeep of its facilities. Prior to that, he worked as a carpenter and subcontractor, and on the side he would create metal buildings for clients. His accomplishments in carpentry and construction were not limited to financial profit; Lee's father has built his own home more than once, and Lee explained that the house his father lives in is a reflection of his hard work and artistic eye, explaining that the home is "pretty much 95% entirely him. He takes a lot of pride doing it himself." His father's personal shop was modest, lacking a wide "fancy" assortment of equipment, but it had the necessary basic tools—a table saw, jigsaw, and other woodworking and metalworking tools—to be able to complete his construction-related tasks.

"He's always been a do-it-yourself guy," Lee says. "Even in old age, it's hard for him to stop working even though his body can't keep up doing that sort of thing." Growing up, Lee witnessed the hard work and time his father dedicated to various projects, as well as the rewarding fruits of such intense labor from what was once nothing. His childhood was filled with opportunities to help and learn from his father the many ways to create beautiful work with his own hands. "I remember when I was probably six or so, I was making birdhouses. Some kids would have lemonade stands, but I had a little stand in the yard where I'd sell wooden swords and birdhouses."

It's not difficult to see how Lee's life became so seamlessly intertwined with craft making, but I was curious to know: how and why was Prince Armory started? "The simplest explanation of it is that I was introduced to Renaissance Festivals when I was in my middle to late teens, and I hadn't been to one before that, surprisingly. I guess because I lived in a small town in the middle of nowhere and hadn't seen much of the world yet." Lee fell in love with the life and culture of the Renaissance Festivals and became a regular participant. He also became passionate about live-action role-playing and hobbyist costuming. "I saw people running around with suits of armor and I just thought that was the coolest thing," Lee remembers. "So eventually, I decided I had to have one myself and I actually commissioned one and that's kind of where the long story starts."

Through commissioning his own suit, he was able to connect with and apprentice under a leatherworking master. Under that guidance, Lee was able to build his skills in leatherworking and create his own beautiful pieces. He continued to work at his craft and skills, and for the time being he created for the sake of creating. This often included unpaid or noncommissioned pieces to build a body of work that he could display using online social media forums, predominantly DeviantArt. His work spread throughout this artistic community and eventually led to his first orders. At that point, the effort and time he put into the work outweighed the financial benefits of selling it. Despite this imbalanced ratio of labor-to-fee, Lee made his products look their very best, adding incredible detail and artistry that caught the attention of a larger online audience. By continuing this path of producing unique work with high quality and standards, he built a portfolio that eventually led to a larger client base. These new high-spending patrons placed both their money and trust in Lee's craftsmanship, allowing him to push the bar on design possibilities even further. Lee spent his time freely experimenting with different materials and an array of techniques; from there, he created Prince Armory in the summer of 2007. "It started in a small backyard shop with help from great friends and employees, and of course wonderful clients along the way who trusted us with their visions."

IMAGE 9.3 *Work-in-progress for phoenix armor.* Photo courtesy of Samuel Lee.

Lee normally has one to three full-time employees in the Prince Armory shop. He also hires five or six apprentices to work on custom projects, items for stock, special events, and conventions. There are typically several projects happening in the shop concurrently, although Lee questions if this is the most efficient way to work. This pace suits Lee and allows him to bounce from project to project, continuously stimulating his creativity. The typical work process begins with deciding who leads the design—whether it is him, a colleague, or the client/brand. Then they create product pricing and a production timeline. His overall design development does not drastically differ between private clients and commercial ones. Normally, Lee's client will stumble upon an existing piece and want something similar. This is ordinarily the base point of artistic discussion that Lee can reference for questions and ideas.

"I'll try to talk with them, figure out what their goals are, what their preference is, color scheme, and come up with a theme," Lee explains, "I like to organically grow the process and design throughout the process, [adding] layers of complexity and detail until it's the best I can do for that particular project." Other factors such as budget and time also are taken into consideration, so Lee discusses the level of detail each client can expect within their price bracket. After agreements are made, the project is added into his queue, and he alerts the client when construction officially starts on their piece. Lee sends his clients work-in-progress photos to keep them updated and excited as they wait. A basic suit can take up to a week to complete, depending on the skill level of his current crew and the limitations of the budget or materials. An elaborate suit and matching accessories such as a helmet or weaponry can take a few weeks to a few months to complete. Once the construction process is finished, the studio staff photographs and documents each piece before shipping it to the client.

I ask Lee if there was a project that was one of his most challenging or memorable. "Well, I'm not sure which one would be the hardest," he responds. "There's a challenge with each project and even the ones that don't have a challenge

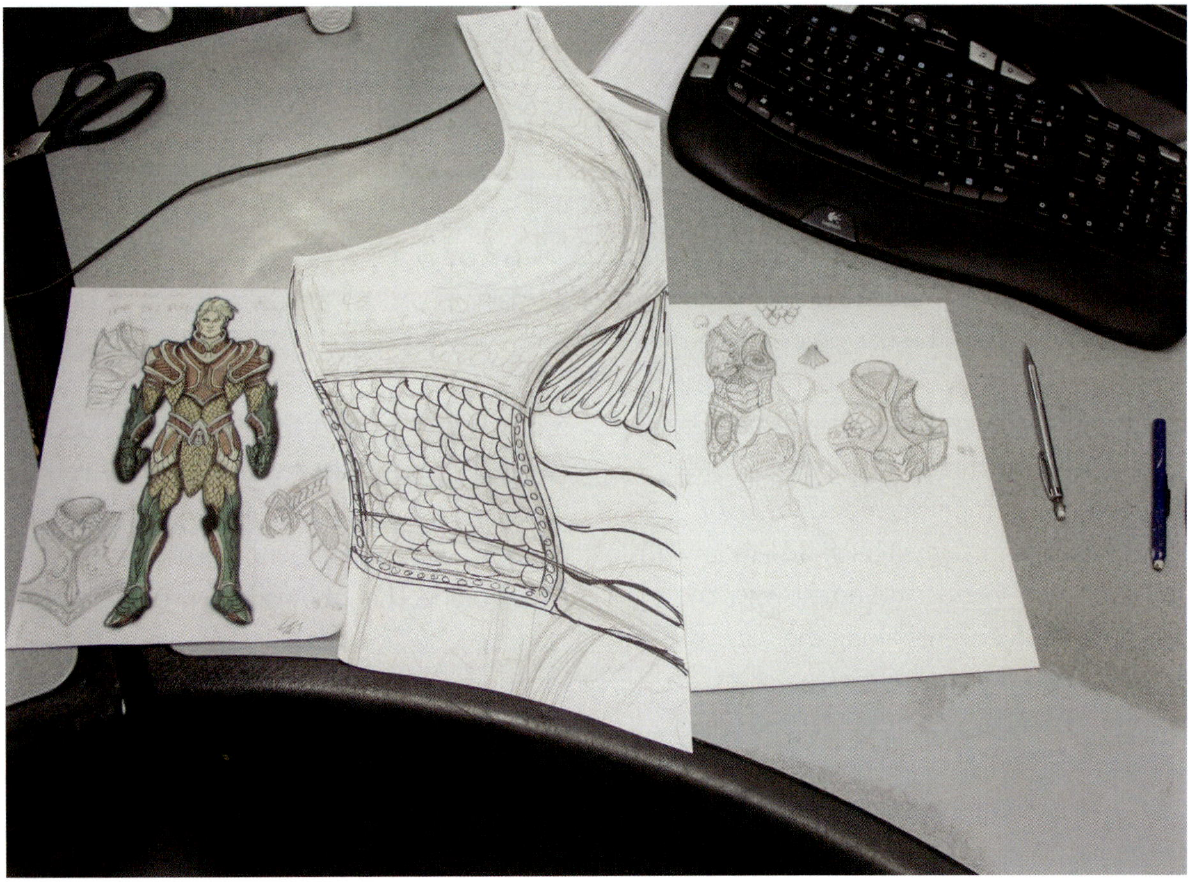

IMAGE 9.4 *Sketch and design process for armor inspired by* Aquaman.
Photo courtesy of Samuel Lee.

IMAGE 9.5 *Completed armor inspired by Aquaman.*
Photo courtesy of Samuel Lee.

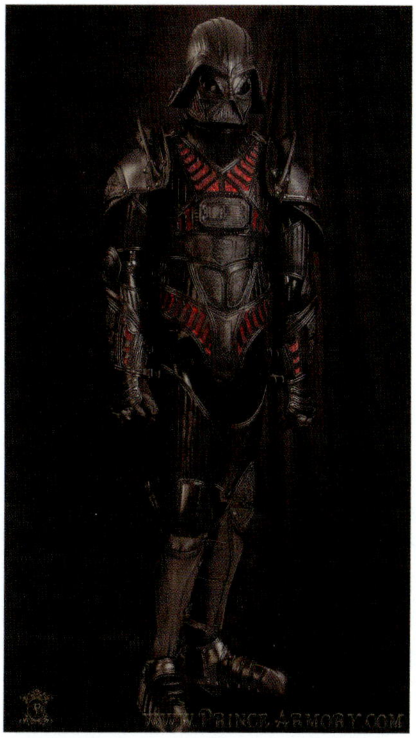

IMAGE 9.6 *Darth Vader–inspired armor.*
Photo courtesy of Samuel Lee.

specifically, I still try to challenge myself to come up with something interesting and unique. Something that's definitely a challenge is some of the medieval superhero spinoffs. Like Darth Vader, for example, it would be pretty easy to do a literal extrapolation in hard leather, but then it would look too much like the movie and then . . . there's no real character to it." Lee challenges himself to find the perfect balance between innovative design and paying homage to original brand imagery. His goal is to create exceptional work that will also please crowds of loyal fans. Lee also aims to create products with a high level of artistry and functionality to accommodate more practical uses. For example, Lee created the armor used for the touring production of *Rodgers + Hammerstein's Cinderella* where it was important that the suit allow the actor to perform with ease. More recently, Lee created a suit featured in a Samsung Smart TV commercial in which the character rides a galloping horse while wearing a custom made elven knight armor suit. Often there is pressure to invest more time, energy, and creativity for the higher-budget and higher-profile pieces to make them "stand out even more. The iconic superheroes, like Iron Man or Batman, for example—you can't mess

IMAGE 9.7 Cinderella *armor.*
Photo courtesy of Samuel Lee.

IMAGE 9.8 *Elven knight armor.*
Photo courtesy of Samuel Lee.

those up! You can't botch those, or you'll be known for that!" Lee jokes with an air that is both humorous and serious, showing pride for his work and awareness he must constantly challenge himself to achieve continued success.

So, what's next for Prince Armory? What keeps Samuel Lee dedicated and excited about the work he is doing with his team? Lee would like to be more involved with commercial projects, possibly theatre, television, or film. "I would like to be part of whatever becomes the next *Game of Thrones* because I feel like I have a lot I can contribute in respect to designs," he says, "especially if it's some sort of fantasy medieval, because that's definitely my niche." Lee also adds, "But I'm also very content with my private clients and occasional commercial projects as well. So I mean, I can't complain, is basically what I'm saying. If it maintains, it's still really good as far as I'm concerned."

(Editor's note: Lee created a blog entry, "Making Medieval Superheroes—The Leathercraft of Samuel Lee," for the Stan Winston School of Character Arts (accessible through StanWinstonSchool.com) that describes his work process. Lee can also be found through his DeviantArt profile.)

ARTIST BIO

Samuel Lee is founder and design lead for Prince Armory, located in Houston, Texas. He discovered a love of fantasy armor through early experiences with Renaissance Fairs and cosplay events. Lee creates custom armor, costumes, props, and weapons for film, television, and theatrical productions, as well as commissions for private clients and collectors. Recent projects include elven knight armor for a Samsung Smart commercial, the national tour of *Rodgers + Hammerstein's Cinderella*, and the warrior armor for the *Dark Avenger 3/Darkness Rises* game. For more information about Lee, please consult his website www.princearmory.com.

CHAPTER 10

JUST DIVE IN

An Interview With Paul Huntley

Leslie Stamoolis

IMAGE 10.1 *Paul Huntley outside his Upper West Side studio in New York.*
Photo courtesy of Paul Huntley.

You have seen his work. If you've seen the original *Cats*, *Evita*, *Amadeus*, or *Mamma Mia!* you've seen his work. If you've seen *The Producers*—onstage or on film—you've seen his work. If you've seen Glenn Close or Patti LuPone in almost anything, you have seen Paul Huntley's work. Paul Huntley, master wig designer and maker, was presented the Tony Award for Excellence over fifteen years ago for designing and crafting wigs for hundreds of productions on Broadway. But his body of work on stage, film, and television has only continued to grow, and in the last three years alone he has opened ten shows, one of which is still running (*Prince of Broadway*) and one of which is now touring the country (*A Bronx Tale, The Musical*). Of course, he didn't work the entire twentieth century—"Most people think I did!" he laughs—but his firsthand knowledge of the changing aesthetics and techniques of wig and hair design is most impressive.

What keeps him going show after shows? A simple question, one often asked of those who demonstrate longevity in a field. His answer is characteristically clear and heartfelt: "Because I love the craft, you see. I'm absorbed into the craft of wig making and hairstyling. I just love it. Simple as that, I just love it." And directors and actors love him, as he has worked with so many of the same artists multiple times.

Why? Huntley says "I think, to be honest, they feel that they are secure. And they know that the result will be what they want themselves. I think it's simply collaboration. I'm a great one for putting anyone, especially young people, at ease."

Huntley was born just outside of London into a tumultuous time, the late 1930s, as a war-torn Europe still recovering from World War I began to face the possibility of a second major conflict. Experiencing the war years as a young child, he recalls, "We were fascinated by all that excitement of the bombs dropping and all the horrific things of war, because we didn't have to go to school." During this time, a great influence in his life was his mother. As a small boy, he remembers watching, enthralled, as his mother applied her makeup and dressed her hair. But it was not just the glamour makeup Huntley observed—his mother was also "an avid movie buff" who always had movie magazines around the house.

"What started me off on my quest was an article on the wonderful Westmores of Hollywood, who did all that make up for the movies," Huntley shares, referring to the famous family whose patriarch, George Westmore, created the first Hollywood makeup department in 1917. Since then four generations of Westmores have worked in film makeup. "They were making a woman who was in her early thirties into various ages until she was one hundred years old. And there were very descriptive pictures, and I thought . . . this was just magic! You know, I watched my mother put paint and makeup on; but this was, I suppose you would say, a theatrical approach. And so I was a little student at that very tender age, and I made up my mind, this was what I wanted to do. Glamour makeup, of course, is very important, even in the theatre, but it was the theatricality that really made me interested in those pictures, seeing all those incredible lines, and painted creases, and prosthetic makeup."

IMAGE 10.2 *Paul Huntley and his mother.* Photo courtesy of Paul Huntley.

Huntley's mother and aunt often swept him along to the movies for an afternoon of what he calls "magic time." He relates, "I was a little boy who should not have gone to the adult movies, but my mother insisted on taking me. She went at least three or four times a week and so I would go when I was meant to go to school sometimes. Yes, it was my education, there's no doubt about it."

He served in the Royal Medical Corps at the age of eighteen for two years as per his conscripted service, and rose to the rank of corporal while stationed in Hanover, Germany. Afterwards, he tried to find an apprenticeship at a film studio to learn more about wigs, but since nearly all the makeup artists and teachers were in the military, apprenticeships simply were not available. So he enrolled in the Royal Central School of Speech and Drama in London. He worked as a repertory actor for a few years and found himself the de facto hair and wig doctor for his troupe. When they rented wigs and facial hair pieces that needed some attention, they always asked Huntley, "thinking I knew more than I did." Between acting jobs, he worked as a dishwasher at Lyons Corner House, a popular chain of eateries in England, and one day he met a fellow actor who told Huntley he had just applied for a job at Wig Creations, the largest theatrical wigmakers in the world at the time. He applied for the job, too, but they had just filled the job with Huntley's actor acquaintance. Fortunately, that actor was soon offered another acting gig, and the spot at Wig Creations was open again—and they called Huntley. He suddenly found himself at the elbow of Stanley Hall, the legendary wig maker.

Stanley Hall, whom Huntley calls "one of those incredible mentors," began his career as a makeup artist at Pinewood Studios with Alexander Korda in the 1930s. World War II interrupted his film career, though poor eyesight kept him from serving overseas. Instead he spent his required service as a chief organizer of Combined Services Entertainment, producing live shows for the troops. After the war, Hall decided to open a theatrical wig company with the expertise, such as ventilation—the art of knotting individual hair strands onto an open-weave lace—that he had learned working in film. It was essentially what Huntley calls "a movie approach to the theatre." Theatrical wigs at that time were, in Huntley's words, "considerably wiggy." They were made with a wide band of fabric across the front that came down over the forehead and eyebrows. Actors then applied pancake makeup and painted eyebrows on over the fabric. Huntley explains, "If you put on a theatrical wig, it wasn't meant to look real. It was just a disguise. When we look at those wigs today, in museums, you think, oh my god, how did anyone ever put these dreadful things on?" The techniques in film wigs were far more realistic-looking due to the close-up nature of the medium.

But it wasn't just the look of the wig that was more realistic; it was adding realistic character details that Stanley approached in a whole new way for theatre. "Stanley brought the very soft, more natural look—in other words, someone could have a slightly untidy hairstyle as if she had just gotten out of bed, whereas up until a certain time in theatre you simply couldn't do that. People would say, oh, it's untidy, it's not right. Even if she'd been sleeping in it for days, it always looked like the most glamorous head of hair. Therefore, he brought the more naturalistic approach to theatrical wigs, including the hairline. The lace that was used in early wigs was nothing like we know today, and he changed that as well. He manufactured a type of lace that had been used in the films for theatre." Our modern sensibility for naturalistic wigs that reflect the reality of the character, blending seamlessly into an actor's own hairline and built on a sturdy but nearly invisible lace, comes directly from this revolution by Stanley Hall.

Huntley collaborated with Hall on some of the most iconic films of the twentieth century and for most of the finest leading ladies of the cinema. "Because of my age, I was very fortunate to have worked with some of the great wonderful people like Vivien Leigh and Larry Olivier and all those wonderful knights and people of the theatre. I think people probably have the same feeling if they work for Sting—but there was something very special about that time." Perhaps most famously, Stanley

IMAGE 10.3 *Stanley Hall, seated, with apprentice Paul Huntley.*
Photo courtesy of Paul Huntley.

Hall created the wigs for Elizabeth Taylor's *Cleopatra* in 1963, a film that remains dear to Huntley's heart, and demonstrates the tension between period accuracy and star power still being played out at that time.

"Elizabeth had, I think, forty-two wigs. All quite dreadful, not a bit period; the 1960s version of Cleopatra. Hall, of course, worked a lot with Elizabeth Taylor. He cut all those wigs for Cleopatra himself, you know; but of course, he cut them into the style and shape of the actual period. And the producers did not like that at all! They wanted her to look like Elizabeth Taylor. And so all those wigs you see with the beads and the jewels on the braids, he cut those beautifully. There was one wig that was called the tassel wig, which was in fact in the shape of the sphinx. And when she moved, each layer tasseled. It was incredible cutting. And they hated that, it wasn't used. And all the other wigs were cut very short. They weren't long at all. And then some of those extraordinary ones where [she is] taking a bath where it looked like a beehive, I've no idea—pure sixties!"

Huntley remembers this part of his career with great fondness and lauds the ability of films to capture forever the work you have done. "Sometimes when I see movies that we both collaborated on, I think, 'Ah, yes. I can see.' That's what's good about movies, of course; in the theatre it doesn't happen so often, but [in film] you can see the results of the care and attention that was labored on something. And if it pleases you, you're happy; if it doesn't of course you're unhappy. But generally, it's a wonderful record that you can keep."

Stanley Hall and his business partner retained ownership of Wig Creations even as he gave Huntley more and more responsibility and authority over the work. By the late 1960s, he had been traveling and working in both the UK and the United States, when one day on set his current leading lady Elizabeth Taylor asked him if he ever did personal wigs. She had a dear friend who wore a wig in everyday life and he was unhappy with his current one, and she thought Huntley's expertise could rescue him. That friend was Mike Nichols. Soon Huntley was also making wigs for Nichols's films and stage productions, such as his acclaimed but controversial *Carnal Knowledge* in 1971, and the 1974 Tony-nominated and Drama Desk Award–winning *Uncle Vanya*. Eventually Mike Nichols sponsored Huntley's emigration to the United States. "I think I felt it was time," he says of the permanent move. "I'd had several offers to come here and it seemed a natural progression. And I think I felt that I would like to open my own company, which is of course what I did."

Huntley had already met and become a trusted colleague to many of the day's leading directors and actors when he received a request from a young drama student at Juilliard. "The fact is, Patti LuPone knew very early in

IMAGE 10.4 *Paul Huntley fits Patti LuPone.* Photo courtesy of Paul Huntley.

her career that she had very fine hair, and she didn't like to be put in theatrical wigs that didn't look like her own hair, when she was meant to look like she had her own hair. And she came to me and asked if I could make her a wig like her own hair, but a little more. But she said, I'm at Juilliard and I won't be able to afford your prices. And I said, well, we can come to some arrangement. She paid me once a month. She still has the wig, bless her heart; of course she keeps all her wigs from her various productions. And the sweetest creature in the world. I knew she was going to be a superstar." From that point on, Patti LuPone has had Paul Huntley written into every single Broadway contract—she does not do a show without his hand on her wigs.

Huntley's pedigree at Wig Creations gave his career its start, but it's his own sensibility and approach that has set him apart. "When Stanley trained me, hairstyles, even though they were more naturalistic, were still stylized. If you were a maid in a shop or a lowly person, it would still look a little too well done, as far as I was concerned. So when I started to take over the business I approached that part of it, which made it look as though she had just got out of bed or she had just braided it herself and there were parts of it that weren't perfect. And one of the most difficult things about that is continuity. We always say, that looks wonderful, it looks so lovely and so natural; now try and do it again! You try and do that eight times a week."

To keep his vision going, Huntley relies on a strong team—both his staff and the actors themselves. "I have several good teams; it depends on how many shows I'm doing, of course. But you have to have the very best person to start with. You have the head hairdresser on the show and I always let her choose her seconds, and thirds, fourth, whatever amount is required. And then, from time to time, I go and do a little Paul Huntley police work—Sergeant Major Police Huntley goes in. I'm not dictatorial, really. I like a certain standard, obviously. But you have to remember everybody sees things differently. If they think that a pin curl is perhaps kinder if it goes a little higher, or the bangs need to be a little thicker to be more flattering, and they say to me, do you mind if we do this or that—I'm all for that.

"I think the most important thing is your actor has to be happy when they go onstage. It doesn't matter how wonderful and creative we are. They are the people who have to look at themselves in the mirror, and let's face it, they see themselves just from the waist up mostly, sitting down in front of their mirror. And if they go on feeling not so wonderful, nothing's ever going to be right. We are psychiatrists, you see. I mean, I can be firm; I can say, well, that wouldn't really work because you're a working-class person from somewhere and this is 1906 or something—you wouldn't look as though you'd just been to the beauty parlor. And that's when I can perhaps be a little firmer. But generally speaking, I don't hammer the whole thing, because they've got to love you as well. Some people know their faces only too well, and they know certain things will not do. And therefore I say, 'Well, I understand, I understand. We'll try it though. Yes, just try it once.' And that's hopefully how we get our way!"

Before the wigs ever reach the actors or the crew, Huntley begins with the script itself and the collaboration with the costume designer. "It's the most important thing of all, dear; I love it. I have to work very carefully and thoroughly with the costume designer. Of course, the clothes maketh the man, don't they? The hair is very important, we know, but at the same time when you're in the theatre you're looking at a full-length body, and so therefore I want to know where they come from and what character they're playing, and usually that's how we start."

Huntley has worked with some of the most notable costume designers of our time, such as William Ivey Long, Ann Roth, and David Zinn. A favorite collaboration was with John Bury on the original *Amadeus*. Bury designed scenery, costumes, and lighting, and was nominated for Tony Awards and Drama Desk Awards for all three areas in 1981. (He won the Tony Awards for his scenic and lighting designs.) "I absolutely adored *Amadeus*. Oh, I loved it. That was divine to work on. That's one of my most favorite periods, the eighteenth century. I like natural hair powdered, isn't that funny. I just think it looks lovely, to have that light dusting of powder other than a very white wig. I mean, you can't always do it, and there are times when a white wig is required. But I try very hard to make sure that I get my powder on. But that's me. I'm having my way."

But "having his way" is not his usual method of working—he is quick to defer to his fellow collaborators, in particular the costume designer. "Of course, she knows much better than I do various parts of the garments and whether it's going to go over the head. Whether you're going to have an authentic sweater without buttons or zippers, which of course doesn't always work. I want the costume designer always to have an input in what she wants her people to look like, because she has a much more overall picture than I do."

It is this graciousness to his fellow artists, and his willingness to learn and evolve, that features again and again in his stories about successful collaborations or how changing methods and technologies have affected his craft. One of the biggest changes, he notes, is the development of high-quality synthetic hair as a viable option: "When it first came on the market, of course I was horrified. I said, oh, good heavens, with human hair you can do whatever you like; with synthetic, you can't. But today, a lot of synthetic wigs are extremely well made. The coloring, the streaking, and the shading have all come into practice, whereas when they first came on the market they literally looked what they were, very fake and not very nice. The fibers have changed. It's not always that terrible shiny look. And of course, I don't use a hard front; naturally we have a lace front on the synthetic wig, so that makes all the difference in the world on the hairline."

Knowing your tools in any craft helps you achieve your goals, and synthetic hairs have become an invaluable tool, as Huntley notes. Human hair is sourced from various places. "It comes from Russia, it comes from Asian countries, and it used to always come from Italy because the nuns would take their vows and sell their hair. So Italy was one of the greatest hair suppliers for wigs in the world, beautiful hair. But the biggest problem today is white hair because you can't get an abundance of natural white hair. It's rare you see light or silver grey hair long, and when you do it's staggering. But that is where synthetic comes into play; you can get the most wonderful white fibers that aren't shiny. And you can mix those with human hair, and you can steam it and curl it, and its absolute perfection . . . It's the old story, isn't it—once we have knowledge, you can fly, as they say. And with certain styles, for instance that bob that Millie had, with the type of tap dancing in *Thoroughly Modern Millie*, it had to be something that fell back absolutely into that bob. And so synthetic was the best way to go."

Consistency as well as longevity are important factors when shows run as long as Huntley's have—for example, eighteen years for *Cats* or fourteen years for *Mamma Mia!* Styling, lighting, and dancing all contribute to a wig's slow demise so the team that maintains the wigs is vitally important. "You have to have a very wonderful staff," he says. "People who really know how to look after them and block them correctly so that it doesn't stretch or fray, because lace today is much more refined, but it still needs to be taken care of. But they can last very, very long—literally years." Wigs for the six-year run of *The Producers* lasted the entire time Huntley says, lauding his staff's work.

IMAGE 10.5 *Paul Huntley fits Sutton Foster for* Thoroughly Modern Millie.
Photo by Sara Krulwich.

Generally, Huntley is known for his natural, highly realistic looks, though shows like *Hairspray* or a recent *Henry IV* at Shakespeare Theatre Company are occasional forays into the fantastical. The greatest example of fantasy wig styling is his masterpiece *Cats*. "It was such an extraordinary experience, because it wasn't like anything we'd ever seen before. It looked very much like the Japanese theatre because they use a lot of that type of stylization . . . it was just glorious in all those colors." To achieve those iconic looks, Huntley turned to an old standby for facial hair due to its coarseness—yak. "You could do many things with it; you could pull it out and make those ears and it behaved beautifully, and—as we talk about continuity—it stayed in place. When you get it from the animal, it's not anything like the final result—it has to be processed, it has to be cleaned, and it has to be bleached white. And then you are able to dye those extraordinary colors, because the bleached white hair is very clear and clean and takes to the dye." He also notes that he uses natural dyes like logwood, madder, and cutch almost as often as chemical dyes; both human and synthetic hair take well to both natural and chemical dyes, he says. "This business of continuity—you have to have a formula. You can experiment and do wonderful things, but if you are going to make something that has to be used eight shows a week, it has to be consistent. And it does fade under the lights."

Huntley acknowledges the evolutions in theatrical lighting with a typical quip: "You have to sell your soul to the lighting person, don't you?" Not only does lighting affect the wig's lifespan, it must be considered when choosing colors. "You always have to remember that with a top light on top of their heads, it's going to be very intense. And so I shade my wigs very much, that's the one thing that I really brought into play. I never do a flat blonde; I always shade the root."

Another evolution of technology that directly affects his work: "The mic, of course, has changed our world, hasn't it. When we first started out, mic packs were huge! I don't know how the poor people ever kept them on their heads." He is referring to the fact that when an actor wears a mic, the battery pack must be attached to their body somehow. Sometimes it is worn on a belt around the torso, but most sound people prefer the pack to be worn on the actor's head underneath their wig, so the cord is also contained on the head. "In musicals, it's ideal to be in the head because of quick changes—you don't go through all that trouble of the cord [getting tangled]. Of course, as we know, the mic packs now are much smaller. But it is a tough one when you're doing a 1920s very short cut at the nape. I think we are lucky with Edwardian styles and 1940s styles and that, but the 1920s and 1930s are tough with the mic packs, I always think."

When asked if he ever wins the battle of a mic pack placement in a difficult era, Huntley is again gracious: "I win the battle only usually when they want two mic packs in the head. For instance, *Evita*, with that balcony sequence, she always wears two mic packs and it is a terrible problem. But we are lucky in a way that she wears a braid on the nape of her neck, which covers both. The head is much larger than it normally should be, but you have to just say, well, the people in the house won't know the difference."

But for all those changes, Huntley still maintains things haven't changed much—neither the methods themselves nor his approach to it. "There are still people who ventilate, especially in England. And I get very nervous—I'm always nervous about everything I do. But I think that's because one cares about the work so much. I care very much for my craft."

For those interested in pursuing wig making, he stresses the importance of connecting with those who have gone before us. "You dive in!" he advises. "It is a personal connection. I was so fortunate. Stanley Hall was one of those incredible human beings, a master of his work. In my second week, Stanley said 'How are you at painting?' I said, what do you mean, painting? He said 'Oh, well, I've got a hundred wigs that have to have gold leaf painting on them for a special thing.' And that was the first time I had touched wigs at Wig Creations . . . Yes, you dive in."

"I think you will find today people are more aware of wigs and what they can do," Huntley muses, as he considers his field's future. "Because of all the films being made today, you can see the most extraordinary wigs. But they still don't have a separate Academy Award for hair. It's makeup." For that matter, the Tony Awards do not have any category honoring makeup, hair, or wigs. If they did, undoubtedly Paul Huntley would have a shelf full.

ARTIST BIO

Paul Huntley began his career as a wig maker and hair designer over forty years ago, working for the legendary Stanley Hall at Wig Creations in the UK, where he learned the history and traditions of hairstyles throughout the ages.

Huntley began his New York career in 1971 when he made wigs for the Mike Nichols's production of *Uncle Vanya*. He worked on both sides of the Atlantic until Nichols suggested that Huntley create a permanent business in New York. This launched a career spanning more than two hundred Broadway shows, as well as film and television productions. His better-known shows include wigs and hair for *Cats*, *Amadeus*, *My Fair Lady*, *Hairspray*, *Evita*, *Dreamgirls*, *Chicago*, *Cabaret*, and *A Bronx Tale, the Musical*.

Huntley has worked with the some of the most legendary leading ladies of the cinema, ranging from Bette Davis, Mae West, Marlene Dietrich, and Vivien Leigh to Jane Fonda, Faye Dunaway, Glenn Close, and Jessica Lange. In 2002, Huntley was awarded the Drama Desk Lifetime Achievement Award, followed in 2003 with the Tony Honor for Excellence in the Theater Award. To learn more about Paul Huntley, visit his website at www.paulhuntleywigs.com.

CHAPTER 11

HATS OFF TO ARNOLD LEVINE!

Martha A. Marking

IMAGE 11.1 *Arnold S. Levine, milliner.* Courtesy of Martha Marking.

On June 8, 2017, I met with milliner Arnold S. Levine at his bustling studio on 8th Avenue in the Garment District in New York City. Levine's workshop is an eclectic collection of millinery supplies as well as memorabilia from shows gone by. The day I visited his employees were busily working on multiple projects, including hats designed by Bob Mackie for the upcoming *The Cher Show* opening at the Neil Simon Theatre in November 2018; crowns for a promotional video for an upcoming motion picture about Freddie Mercury; and a yet-to-open Broadway production of *Moulin Rouge!* with costumes designed by Catherine Zuber. The atmosphere was comfortable and inviting, and Levine was gracious and jovial. If only the walls could talk! I'm sure they'd regale us with stories of Broadway shows gone by and scintillating conversations between Levine and the renowned designers with whom he has worked.

If you have been in regular attendance at Broadway shows during the past twenty years, you have undoubtedly seen Levine's work. He has worked on nine productions that have won Tony Awards for Best Costume Design including 2019's *Bob Mackie's The Cher Show* and seventeen productions that have been nominated.

IMAGE 11.2 *Employee working on Mackie's design for* The Cher Show.
Courtesy of Martha Marking.

Levine grew up in Connecticut to a mother who had, prior to being a homemaker, been an English teacher and a father who was a doctor, a general practitioner. He cheerfully recounted writing plays and acting in them when he was in the third grade. Levine recalled "always being interested in art and theatre" since his parents had taken him to "quite a bit of theatre" when he was young due to their proximity to New York City. When he was "trying to decide what he was going to do when he grew up," he determined that the repetition involved with acting did not appeal to him. Theatre technology, he thought, might be a better fit. Levine explained that he went to Carnegie Mellon University, studying first as a set designer but later finding inspiration from costumers Barbara and Cletus Anderson who "kind of lit a fire" in him. When he took Barbara's patterning class, the work was "so intuitive" for him that he "knew he was meant to do this." He also recounted that if he'd have known that he was going make hats for a living he would have "paid more attention" to geometry in high school.

After we spoke about his background I asked Levine specific questions about his work, career path, and his advice for young designers and technicians.

MM: Barbara and Cletus were your mentors and they helped you develop your interest in costumes. Was there a moment that it "clicked," when you shifted to millinery as a focus?

AL: Ok . . . I have a weird "lucky streak," and I know it, and I am very grateful for it. At this point I had taught for a while [*at Western Illinois University*] and was doing regional theatre and dinner theatre. When I moved to New York in 1980, a friend who I had gone to school with called and asked what I knew about millinery. I told her I had "made some hats but didn't have much experience, why?" She said, "I'm working up at New York City Ballet and they need a milliner." I said, "I'm not a milliner." She said, "Shut up and get up here." So, I interviewed for a production of *Cinderella* for Chicago Ballet that was being designed by Ben Benson. Suzanne Farrell was dancing Cinderella and her husband, Paul Mejia, was choreographing. They hired me on because they did not need "HAT" hats. In other words, there was a lot of "nontraditional" millinery in that production. They sat me down with their milliner—who I thought was looking at my technique with abject horror! [*He laughed.*] I found out later that she was impressed with the speed of my work, because I did end up staying there for a while. She was a *trained* milliner, and she said "I couldn't do what you're doing because is not my training." Ben Benson then asked me to be his assistant at City Ballet. So now I've been in New York less than a half of a year, and I'm assisting the man who was designing most of the new productions at City Ballet at that time. While I was there I met Florence Klotz. She came in to design a ballet with her own assistant, but after a short time I became *her* assistant as well as Ben's. I did another show with her, and when I left the Ballet I ended up working with her on a number of Broadway shows.

So, one thing kept leading to another. I started sending out resumes as a milliner and, as this "weird luck thing" would have it, I went to a party hosted by the guys who had just purchased Penn and Fletcher [*a well-established custom embroidery company*]. There was a designer at the party who was designing for New York City Opera. He was looking at resumes for an open position and because he had just met me at this party said, "Why don't we have him do some hats for us?" That got me started with the Opera.

After the second or third show I did for New York City Opera, they agreed that they would find me a place to work. So, I went to Grace Costumes. They had a milliner who died, and who they had never replaced. Grace Miceli and Maria Brizzi, who I consider to be my fairy godmothers, owned Grace Costumes and said, "We have a millinery room and we like you, would you be interested in doing this?" At this point I'm still basically a designer and doing millinery in my free time. But this offer came up and I thought, why not? [*Raised his hands questioningly.*]

MM: Serendipitous!

AL: I went to work for them but we eventually became two separate companies under the same roof. This worked out very nicely, and by the time I moved out on my own I had a decent client base. One thing led to another, and now twenty years, or whatever years later, this is my business.

MM: What differences, if any, are there in how you work now compared to how you worked when you were just starting out? Any new materials or methodologies? I think about how lighting, sound and scene shifting have changed . . . has millinery?

AL: This is a many fold but simple answer. The basic way we build a hat has not changed. The materials have changed because many of the older materials are not being made any more. Many kinds of plastics are available now but there is a learning curve to working with them. More of what you need has to be purchased from out of town—double buckram, for example, can only be custom ordered. I do a lot more buying on online.

MM: Well, the ability to order online is one change.

AL: There is online. But also, it is not in town. A lot of it just isn't here anymore.

MM: Yes, I was reading that you were heavily involved in trying to save New York's Garment District.

The Garment District, in its heyday, was located in Manhattan between 7th and 9th Avenues and 35th to 42nd Streets. It employed and housed several hundred craftspeople as well as manufacturers of fabric and supplies. Anything needed for a vibrant fashion industry could be found there.[1]

MM: There was a quote that I read that you said something to the effect, "this should have been started twenty years ago when it had already been a dire situation".[2]

AL: How do you move the district after two thirds of it has already dispersed? The mayor came up with this great idea and if they would have said, "how about a bunch of you move here?" It might have made sense. But there still would have been a problem for theatre. In the beginning I don't think the garment people thought theatre had anything to do with them. They felt what they were doing was a totally different thing. At this same time [*2007*] there was a stagehands' strike which lasted quite a while and their fabric sales went down. I talked with someone in the District and he said that he finally realized, "if we have a bride come in we'll have a salesman who'll be busy with that bride for six hours and she'll buy $1,000 worth of fabric. I can have theatre people come in for fifteen minutes and spend $1,000. Theatre people come in, do their thing and go. You know what you want. It's there, it's not there, you move on. You're not tying people up."

MM: Are there new materials that you enjoy working with more than others? Are there some that have had a higher learning curve?

AL: There are all kinds of them, and I'm still in the middle of the learning curve. There are things I want to play with, but I stay busy enough that I don't have time to just play. Some materials are *so* expensive that you can't afford to play with them. If you have a client waiting for something and it doesn't work, you're back to square one.

MM: How do you describe what you do to people outside of the industry? Not the job title necessarily, although maybe you want to go there too, but the basic artistry of your work?

AL: Sometimes, depending on whether or not I think they'll follow what I'm doing, I say that we make hats for people that don't exist. This is a variation of a quote from a friend of mine who used to say she "makes clothes for people who don't exist." [*He chuckles.*] I basically say we make hats for theatre. I start there and then I branch out. We have done movies, television, theatre, cruise ship entertainments, and parades. Anything you need to put a hat on, we've probably done.

MM: Is there something you feel that people who don't work in your field should understand about it? Are there misconceptions that you find you need to address?

AL: I think all of theatre needs to be explained somewhat. For example, you can't go to the restoration store and buy clothes. I think it's that simple. Most people don't understand what we do because it simply doesn't occur to them where these things come from.

MM: And the patterning and locating fabric . . .

AL: Yeah, it's all those things. In their minds, when I explain it, it is a variation on shopping.

MM: Do you do samples? Mock-ups? Renderings? How do you communicate what you are thinking with the designers and craftspeople working with you?

AL: Designers usually bring us sketches of what they want. They can be very, very specific, or very, very general. It depends a lot on the drawings of the designer and how much research they bring. Some designers will bring in small sketchy type drawings with beautiful research. Other designers will come in and say, "I want a hat this color. I want a four inch flower on it and I want this color ribbon." Everything is totally laid out.

MM: So in that instance you're a technician?

AL: Yes. There are many different layers to this. They might even ask, "Why did you do this or that?" And I'll say, "Well, that is what was in your drawing." They sometimes ask me why I look at their drawings!

I always used to do mock-ups. Now we do shows with so little lead time that there really is no time. What I may do though, if the designer likes the mock-up, is to use it for the lining.

MM: Has your lead-time gotten shorter?

AL: Way shorter. When I started out we would usually have six to eight weeks in the costume shop. Now we're lucky if we get four weeks. Producers equate lead-time with money, and it is not really that at all. What you're paying for is the hat. If we have seven weeks to do a hat they'd get a better hat than if we've had three days. We're rushing to get it done. But they need it now, now, now!

MM: Do you think they recognize quality?

AL: No, the producers don't because they don't see it. They're not ever that close to it.

MM: When you are working with a designer, how does your communication with them work after you've gotten their designs in your shop?

AL: It depends a lot on the designer. With some designers you speak a very similar language, and with other ones, you don't. I have been a designer, and I work with designers. I know how busy they are and trying to fit me in is not necessarily easy. They have other things to do before they deal with me. They may not even know what the clothes look like yet. I try to be as prepared for them as I can. I don't want to waste their time. If I have seen their sketches and I know what they want me to do, I will probably pull out feathers, flowers and fabrics. Things they might like, because if it's here in the shop, we can start. If it isn't, they can look at it and say, "I love this color. I hate the fabric, but I love the color." Now I have a direction to go in.

IMAGE 11.3 *Hat tree in Levine's studio.*
Courtesy of Martha Marking.

MM: I was always taught to not show a director anything that you wouldn't want to put on stage. If you don't like it, don't show it to them.

AL: Right. And part all of it is that they don't have to use any of what I have. If they would like to, it is here. I had a designer who never wanted to pull anything out of my stock because "somebody had already used it." I explained to him that if other people are out swatching today seven of them could put the same fabric on their Broadway show. If it's in my shop, and I've had it for twenty years, nobody else is going to have it.

MM: Do they get that?

AL: Yes, after a while they do, and then they ask me what I've got. I do a lot of work with Cathy Zuber, and she loves that I will pull things out of my hidey-holes for her. This pile of stuff [*motions to the end of the table*] is for a new headpiece that got added to *Moulin Rouge!* She doesn't have to use any of it but if she likes it, it's here and we can get it started.

MM: Since you have a background as a college professor, I wonder, do you teach millinery classes?

AL: At the moment I am an adjunct instructor at SUNY-Purchase. I do a millinery class each fall for the seniors. I have been teaching there for four years. I've also taught a Design I course there and, I must say, I really love teaching

IMAGE 11.4 *Headdress for Mackie's design for* The Cher Show.
Courtesy of Martha Marking.

design, which I do all the time but not in a specific way.

MM: As I was preparing for this interview I read several comments from people that have been in your shop. It seems like you are very gracious with your knowledge.

AL: Well, I was a teacher when I started so there is still a huge chunk of teacher in me. Although, having done this for so long, I don't have the teacher vocabulary as handy as I used to. When I worked at City Ballet the people in the shop didn't talk to each other. It was all secrets and that disturbed me greatly.

I do hire people from a wide range of backgrounds. Some of them have been trained as milliners, some as costume designers, and I even had a sculpture major. One of the people who works for me now is a textiles major. Basically, good design is good design no matter what you're designing. Millinery skills can be taught if you've got the patience and general sewing skills. It's a matter of a brain shifting.

MM: Have you noticed differences in the skill levels of recent graduates?

AL: Schools have finally realized that they should be training technicians as well as designers. There was a while there when they only trained designers. If you were in a good school, you learned a lot of technical skills to go along with your design skills. But in their minds, you were not living up to your potential if you weren't designing.

MM: Like this type of work is secondary?

AL: Yes.

MM: What do you recommend for practitioners just starting out? What are some things you feel they should work on or classes they should take?

AL: Most schools don't leave a whole lot of leeway with regard to electives. If you're not a theatre major, you probably can't even get into theatre classes. I don't know if at your school a science major could take a costume construction class . . .

MM: Yes, they can.

AL: A lot of other places they can't because it doesn't work out right. There is also so much online, if a person can learn that way. YouTube videos will show you how to use different supplies and techniques. If you want to make something there is no reason you can't find the information you need online. You may not have the skills at this point, but at least you'd learn what skills you need. Something I always say to people is to learn "stuff." I don't care what you're learning. If you're going to work in a shop, you spend a lot of time with each other. The more you read, the more you watch, the more you learn, the more interesting the conversation is so you don't stultify sitting here.

Also, I may see a new product on TV that has nothing to do with what we are working on and all of a sudden we'll be using it for another purpose. We did a bunch of work for a company called *Slim Goodbody*. They visited schools and talked about the human body. I started using information from my biology classes. Anything you learn gets used one way or

IMAGE 11.5 *Trim detail on Zuber's design for* Moulin Rouge!
Courtesy of Martha Marking.

another, you may not even realize it. It's back to that geometry thing. That's not what I thought I would be doing but it's what I do.

MM: Yes, I tell students that they have to do some math when we pattern. Work with fractions . . .

AL: I'll say, strike an arc and they make a face. If you don't pattern draft, when is the last time you needed to divide a curve?

MM: Exactly! How do you choose projects you work on at this stage in your career?

AL: They come to me. I turn things down if I don't have time or think I can't do them. But, if Jane Greenwood wants me to make a hat for Jane Greenwood, I make a hat for Jane Greenwood.

MM: Do you feel that you need to be connected to a designer? Do you say yes more often to a designer you prefer to work with?

AL: The designers I like working with tend to come back more often. The ones I didn't enjoy working with, probably subconsciously know it, and they decide not to come back. I don't think I'm behaving differently, but maybe I am.

MM: If you hear of something coming down the pike, that you'd like to work on, *The Little Foxes*, for example, do you reach out and say I'm really interested in or do they always come to you?

AL: They usually come to me. I'm trying to remember the last time I actually reached out to say that I was interested in something . . .

MM: Because as a young designer you'd be sending out your resume, your portfolio, all that.

AL: At this point . . . this is something I think that goes back to teaching. I'm very nice to assistants because they have a tough job. After a while, it is the assistants who have a lot to do with inviting you to bid. The very first time I worked with Cathy [*Zuber*] was because I had just worked with her assistant on something else. We've done hats for many of the shows she's done since then but it was her assistant that got our foot in the door.

MM: What are some favorite productions you have worked on? When were you were proudest of your work or most enjoyed the process?

AL: I go back to one show because I am so proud of what we did and almost nobody got to see it. It was *Dance of the Vampires*. I had such a good time working on that. There were a lot of beautiful things in it.

MM: Who was the designer?

AL: Ann Hould-Ward. The show was a disaster, but I had fun. People always think you're going to say the most important or the most impressive one.

MM: Or the most recent one?

AL: You always hope your favorite show is the next one. I think the shows I like best are the ones when it's been a collaborative effort, when the designer is letting the shop use their abilities. I have taught costume history and have a pretty good costume history background. If I can't read something on the drawing, I think about what it would be if it were period. I find that a lot of fun.

IMAGE 11.6 *Production bibles in Levine's studio.* Courtesy of Martha Marking.

My favorite part is setting it all up. It's doing the patterns, it's figuring out what we need to get, how we're going to do it. It's all that. By the time we get to making it, I'm happy to let my studio do the majority of the construction.

MM: Because you're on to the next thing.

AL: My brain is already on to the next thing. Right now [*he gestures to the end of the table*] these are bibles for work we're currently doing. We've got *Cher*, a few things left for *Moulin Rouge!* and *Bohemian*

IMAGE 11.7 *Crown for* Bohemian Rhapsody.
Courtesy of Martha Marking.

Rhapsody. And we're doing a project for Disney.

MM: Since you have your own business, how do you navigate the "business" aspect of your job?

AL: With varying degrees of success. [*He laughs.*] I recently went to a payroll system. I guess I'm a control freak. I do the all the bidding and the billing. I don't know how somebody I hired would know how to bill, although they would probably pay more attention to how long it would it really take to build something. There are certain things that I don't care how long it takes, and I can't charge that much for the work. Then there's that whole thing "Are they not going to come back because it's too much money?" or "Do I want to do more work that I'm not going to make money on?" It's always a balancing act. Budgets are not what they used to be and, despite rising costs, they are not going up. People are trying to do more and more with the same amount of money. We're all trying to find ways to balance the budget and the time available. That's all part of the business.

MM: And shipping . . .

AL: Shipping is hugely expensive because you are still paying for dimensional weight. So if we've got a hat that's this big [*motions with his hands*], it costs two hundred-plus dollars to ship because it ships as a sixty-eight-pound package even though it weighs two pounds.

MM: And you hope they don't put a sixty-eight-pound package on it.

AL: Right. That's part of it. My contracts now have more caveats than they used to. They pay for shipping, custom painting and dyeing, flower making, and feather dyeing.

MM: You mentioned geometry earlier. Is there some other training you wish you'd have had earlier in your career?

AL: I think every designer and craftsperson needs a basic accounting class. It doesn't have to be very long or very hard. Just simple stuff. I wish I would have had computer classes but that already happens now.

MM: What other artisans do you collaborate with and what is your approach to working with them?

AL: There is always the question about whether or not the actor's mic pack is going to be in the hair, but I deal primarily with the costume designer on sound issues. I try to work with the hairdresser. If I need to pin in a hat, I need to know what the hair color is. Is there a lace front on the wig? What are the measurements over the wig? Due to tightening schedules, I almost never have the ability to go into a fitting and have a wig there. In fact, I rarely go to fittings. I try to be as thoughtful as I can about what other people have to do within the framework of my time, energy, and brainpower. Everybody is on the same crazy, stupid schedule. Yeah, I can ask the designer a question, but I may not get an answer right away. And, because we don't do fittings anymore, or very rarely, it is difficult. I also don't know what of the designer's work will stay and what will be cut.

MM: Do you have any other advice you'd like to impart? Is there anything else I didn't ask you that you'd like to share?

AL: If it's something you're interested in doing, whatever it is, ask questions. Marty Pakledinaz [*a Tony Award–winning costume designer*] once said—not a direct quote—he told me that people would send him letters and say, "I am an aspiring costume designer or technician. You should hire me. I love your work." He said, "I am not here as a teacher but as a designer. In your letter, tell me what you can do for me as well as what I can do for you."

Meet people. If there is somebody that you are interested in meeting, tell them why. Tell them, I saw your production of this. I would love to meet with you at your convenience, if that would be possible. Nobody gets upset with a little flattery. Let them know if you are doing a show. They're probably not going to go but your name gets across their desk one more time. But don't be a pest. Designers don't have time to meet everybody. It's always a tough thing to put yourself out there. It always has been, but now, in a way, it's even harder because it's so much less personal with texting and all. You can communicate without having real conversations.

I had the most pleasant morning with Levine in his studio. He was so kind to allow me to interrupt his work. His resume is a "who's who" of the most seminal costume designers of the past several decades. He has worked with Desmond Heeley, Theoni Aldredge, Julie Taymor, Martin Pakledinaz, Paul Tazewell, Alvin Colt, Jess Goldstein, Carrie Robbins, and others too numerous to mention. The quality of the work that comes out of his shop is impeccable. He has enabled costume designers to more effectively tell the stories of the characters brought to life on stage, screen, and other venues like cruise ships and circus tents. Levine told me next up was a production of *Beetlejuice* designed by frequent collaborator William Ivey Long, projects for Walt Disney World and Disney Cruise Line, an *Anastasia* tour for Linda Cho, and *Bernhardt/Hamlet* for Toni Leslie James. It all begins again!

IMAGE 11.8 *Hat blocks in Levine's studio.*
Courtesy of Martha Marking.

ARTIST BIO

Arnold S. Levine has, for the last 28 years, been the owner of and run Arnold S. Levine, Inc. Theatrical Millinery and Crafts in New York City. A graduate of Carnegie-Mellon University, he started teaching at Western Illinois University after graduation. From there it was into the world of Indiana Rep, Dinner Theatre, and summer stock. After moving to NYC in 1980, he started designing Off-Broadway and regionally. As a Broadway Assistant/Associate Designer, he assisted Florence Klotz and Patricia Zipprodt, working on four Tony Award-winning shows. At that point he became assistant to the head of the New York City Ballet costume shop, Ben Benson, and began working in ballet and doing millinery for the New York City Opera, eventually opening his own craft studio.

As a costume craftsperson, Arnold and his staff have worked with over 150 major designers. Their work can be seen on Broadway, Off-Broadway, and in opera, ballet, television, movies, and cruise ships around the country and the world.

Arnold is an adjunct teacher at SUNY Purchase College and is the co-author, with Robin L. McGee, of *Patterns for Costume Accessories*.

NOTES

1. Appleton, Jean. "Opinion | Long Live the Garment District." *The New York Times*, August 1, 2012. *NYTimes.com*. www.nytimes.com/2012/08/02/opinion/long-live-the-garment-district.html.
2. Otis, Ginger Adams. "Broadway's Hat Maker Hopes City Preserves What's Left of the Garment District—NY Daily News." *Nydailynews.Com*. new-york/star-hat-maker-hopes-left-garment-district-remains-article-1.3089263. Accessed September 2, 2018.

CHAPTER 12

STANLEY ALLAN SHERMAN

Carving His Own Path

Michael Vincent

IMAGE 12.1 *Stanley Allan Sherman holding a ManKind mask and a second backup mask for the World Wrestling Federation, just before the finishing stage in 1996.*
Courtesy of Stanley Allan Sherman.

> "A journey of a thousand miles begins with a single step."
>
> —Chinese philosopher Lao-zi

This quote seems perfectly fitting to the story of Stanley Allan Sherman, who has been around the world to discover his passion. A journey that started in Portland, Oregon, went through the Middle East and Europe, and while he may have landed in New York City his discoveries along the way reach all over the globe.

Stanley continues his journey in the rediscovery and furthering of the techniques used in the field of mask making and theatre arts performance in general. Always up for a challenge, and prepared for possible failure, he continually explores and hasn't lost his passion for doing what he loves.

STARTING THE JOURNEY

As children, we often see the world as a place of wonder and possibilities as we are exposed to many different things that come across our paths. Stanley Allan Sherman was no different. His wonder for the performing arts started at his family home in Portland, Oregon, first watching episodes of *The Ed Sullivan Show* in which he was delighted to see dancers, comics, and all sorts of variety acts televised and making a living out of having fun. He would go on to pursue his creative outlet in theatre ever since,

IMAGE 12.2 *Stanley Allan Sherman having some fun wearing one of his Commedia dell'arte Zanni masks.* Courtesy of Stanley Allan Sherman.

from kindergarten on. Instead of merely copying things that he saw on television, as many of his classmates were prone to do, Stanley had a desire to create and be original.

Growing up with four other siblings (two brothers and two sisters), a mother and father who both worked, and a tight budget, Stanley would often need to be creative in his play, particularly at Halloween time. Oftentimes he and his brothers would make their Halloween costumes and masks from whatever they could find lying around. The one time that his father bought him a mask from the store, at Stanley's pestering, it failed to hold the same joy that the ones he had created from scratch had held, further cementing his desire to be wholly original. Stanley would continue this desire to experiment and create throughout his career.

The arts run deep within the Sherman family, as Stanley has a sister who is a union costumer and a grandfather who was a tailor. However, Stanley credits his father in encouraging him to follow his dreams. Irv Sherman, Stanley's father, was a jazz pianist when he was drafted to serve during World War II. Loving his music so much, Mr. Sherman brought with him a harmonica and sheet music, schlepping them with him throughout the jungle fighting and war conditions that were to come. Afterwards Mr. Sherman received a full scholarship to the Juilliard School of Music in New York City.

The advice Irv Sherman, out of concern, got from his father, in regards to his music, was "Stop this nonsense and go get a real job." As Stanley left to discover his path in the world his own father had a different piece of advice to give his son Stanley. The advice Mr. Sherman gave to Stanley was "Do not look back," encouraging words for anyone who must discover their path, or in Stanley's case, forge his own path.

When asked if he ever did look back, Stanley's reply is simply, "No."

DESTINY IN THE DESERT

After high school Stanley went off to save the world, but the journey would end up saving him. He was mentored by Lionel and Hans Killner in Tel Aviv, who would be his guides toward dance, mime, and discovery of what he would be destined to do. He then planned to go on to Paris to study with Marcel Marceau, but plans can often be rerouted by happy chance, as he discovered while hitchhiking in Israel by the Dead Sea. It was getting late, and not wanting to spend the night in the desert, Stanley came across a driver who was willing to give a ride to some of the trio that he was with, but alas she only had room for two passengers. Stanley decided to create his own path, and by simply saying "I am skinny," he squeezed himself into her vehicle and made room for himself. As they made their way to the youth hostel in the oasis Ein Gedi, the driver, out of boredom, asked Stanley what it was that he was doing here. He informed this stranger of his plan to move to Paris and study mime under Marcel Marceau. The stranger, not knowing Stanley at this time, proceeded to tell Stanley that he should not go there, but that he needed to study at the Ecole Jacques Lecoq for theatre mime movement and then proceeded confidently to list the reasons why.

IMAGE 12.3 *The S&M Horse Head ballet dancer's mask for Company XIV, Dance Inc., 2015 production of* Cinderella, *Zane Pihlstrom, costume designer.*
Courtesy of Stanley Allan Sherman.

The magic of this interaction and the happenstance of destiny made the encounter special to Stanley, and he would go on to study at the Ecole Jacques Lecoq from 1970 to 1972, where, as fate would have it, he really discovered performance and masks.

CARVING HIS OWN PATH

Looking back, Stanley has some advice for those starting out on their journey of discovering what it is that they really want to do: "Is it what you love and care about? Go for it. Do not fear making your own market for yourself, striking out on your own. Figure out how to do it so it pays your rent and bills."

"Jobs are not always handed to you. After you finish your education, your real education begins . . . Find the best mentors for you. The best teachers in the world help . . . If you do an internship, do not expect to start out doing great things. The struggle and the journey is very much a part of your base that you build . . . Understanding that failure is not failure, it is a piece of the process and a guide to direct you to doing something successfully."

While in school in Paris he slept in a van with several other people, modeled for the master's sculpture classes at Ecole Nationale Superieure des Beaux-Arts, and performed on the streets in order to feed himself. Stanley's mask-making journey started with him making masks out of necessity for his own shows. His first paid job as a mask maker came years later, and it was for his mentor in New York City, Vasek Simek, and the Perry Street Theater. He was commissioned to make two masks of comedy tragedy skulls for the play *Faust*. He found himself able to make these masks due to the path he had carved for himself by performing his own solo shows and working alongside puppeteers in Portland, Oregon. He learned from them advanced techniques for papier maché, a malleable mixture of paper and glue, or paper and specialty glue, that becomes hard when dry. This was back in 1975 or 1976, and because of their quality he still has them today.

As a mask artisan, due to his experience as a performer, mask-making jobs slowly started to come his way. In 1980 the New York Baroque Dance Company became the first dance company to commission masks to be made for their dancers. Thirty-eight years later the masks are still in use as part of their repertory. The New York Baroque Dance Company may have been the first, but they were certainly not the last.

Stanley credits the S&M Horse Head, made for Company XIV, Dance Inc., as likely being one of the finest mask he has ever created. Understanding what a performer needs to achieve while wearing the mask is vital to Stanley's success. In the case of the S&M Horse Head, the ballet dancer needed to be free enough to move completely, to be able to see clearly, and of course to be able to breathe while wearing the mask. On top of all that it had to give the energy of a real living horse, complete with real horse hardware and S&M hardware. Thinking outside the box and carving his own path, Stanley spent a lot of time listening to his friend David Geyer from Celebration Farms, Maryland, so that he could thoroughly understand the ears, nose, and jaw of a horse's head and the elemental workings of how they all fit together.

IMAGE 12.4 *Newly designed performer's slapstick made from oak.*
Courtesy of Stanley Allan Sherman.

PATHS ARE RARELY STRAIGHT

As a designer, to limit oneself to one thing can, in turn, limit one's marketability. Stanley, always looking for originality and continuing to forge his own path, hasn't limited himself to making masks solely for dance companies, or for theatrical productions for that matter. He has had several notable projects that each presented him with a different challenge and a new skill to develop. Stanley has worked with street performers, rap artists, clowns, pro wrestlers, and, yes, actors and dancers.

IMAGE 12.5 *Philippe Petit taking the top hat for the first trial spin once it had been created for him.*
Courtesy of Stanley Allan Sherman.

Stanley has devoted decades to reinventing the performer's slapstick, mimicking the lost versions of the 1500s. The slapstick is used onstage during Commedia dell'arte shows and creates a loud whack with just a tap. He dove into the finer points of engineering this device with no springs and two pieces of wood. He has since successfully sold them to performers and companies, including his first collegiate sale to Dr. Laura Stafford at Lamar State College in Port Arthur, Texas, who called the slapsticks "The hit of the show."

He created a distressed, old-looking leather top hat for Philippe Petit that took six months to make and was developed out of one piece of leather, stretching it so there would be no cuts or seams, which facilitated Philippe being able to spin the hat on his finger for a prolonged time. The leather-stretching technique has become a signature item in Stanley's creative arsenal. One that he had to develop himself.

He has worked with the World Wrestling Federation as well. He created the Mankind mask for Mick Foley, developing a free-floating moveable jaw so he could still talk and fully embody his character. Originally, the World Wrestling Federation wanted a *Silence of the Lambs*–type of mask, but Stanley informed them that he would not produce something that was the work of someone else, reaffirming his desire to be wholly original. Instead he asked probing questions to get at the heart of what emotions they wanted in this character and developed from there. He has also created the Abyss mask worn by Chris Park with TNT Wrestling. For pro wrestler Magnos he delivered a high-end mask that has options for the character, developing a system of five adjustable straps that go through an adjustable over-the-head strap.

IMAGE 12.6 *The Abyss mask in the works for pro-wrestler Chris Park with TNT Wrestling.* Courtesy of Stanley Allan Sherman.

Another direction Stanley's path has taken him is his custom-fitted leather clown noses, first for his solo shows and then branching out from there. Leather noses are very important for performers who must wear the piece for longer periods; leather noses are easier to breathe through than store-bought plastic noses, which oftentimes have the nose holes anywhere but under the nostrils. A custom-fit leather clown nose is also more comfortable because it fits smoothly and the leather does not sweat like plastic does. There is a clown in Belgium who is very thankful to Stanley for creating a custom-fitted leather clown nose that fits his large nose, allowing him to go on with his work in hospitals.

A job for Stanley can take anywhere from hours to months. After a custom clown nose fitting took five hours to complete, he decided to raise his prices. Oftentimes people don't understand or have a misconception of what it is that designers are actually doing when creating a piece. To that he says, "Everything takes time. Yes, we can rush things. But you need to pay us not to sleep. Custom things can be

IMAGE 12.7 *Set of finished Commedia dell'arte neoprene latex masks waiting to be shipped to their adventures with students and performers.*
Courtesy of Stanley Allan Sherman.

unique. There is a lot in it to make the magic work."

EMOTIONAL COLORS

In order to bring forth the magic within his work, Stanley is very organic in his process. He needs to connect with the person for whom he is creating the mask for, in one way or another, so that it will fit the performer not only physically but on a spiritual level as well. According to Stanley, "Masks do not hide the face. They expose the soul of the performer. A great mask will free the performer to go to places where they have not gone. My job is that . . . Understanding all the above and combining the engineering functioning of a mask with the full character and the room for the performer to fill out all their emotional colors, traveling to depths they would not normally go."

Allowing performers to reach into themselves to reveal their emotional and spiritual colors and then giving that to the audience is incredibly important to Stanley: "If you fill in all the spaces . . . colors, details, etc., there is no room for the imagination." He began learning of people's emotional colors at Ecole Jacques Lecoq and later from Richard Pachinko, and has since expounded this into his own personal philosophy that he works into each piece he creates.

Certain colors are naturally viewed as holding or representing certain emotions or feelings: blue for sadness or energy, red for passion or anger, perhaps yellow for happiness or cowardice. But what emotional color do we, as designers, impart to the things we create? If, as a designer, you are not invested in a certain project or your mind is elsewhere while working, what part of your energy is going to be portrayed to the audience through your creative design, blocking the emotional color, or energy, the performer is trying to convey on stage? Stanley notes, "As artisans we have to be aware of this. We put our energies into what we create."

LESSONS ALONG THE WAY

When Stanley decided to first start making masks, with a particular focus of Commedia dell'arte, few resources were available to him. There were no teachers, and even fewer written materials, on how to create Commedia dell'arte masks. He would have to rediscover many of the techniques that had been lost to history or develop new techniques to achieve his design. Stanley is always on the lookout for new materials to try, and continues taking classes to further his artistry, even after being in this industry for more than forty years: "When I take a class to do something new and different, it is like a vacation!"

Experimentation and learning from failures have been a cornerstone to Stanley's success. However, he cautions all designers, artisans, and fabricators to take into consideration the most important aspect of any design—the designers themselves. In other words "YOU." Stanley notes, "Several young artists from the 1960 and 1970 had all kinds of health problems. Some of those artists are still suffering." He strongly advocates caution whenever working on a project and investing in protective equipment, such as a high-quality respirator with an air filter and eye protectors that wrap around the face. "The price of a good respirator is a lot cheaper than the test a doctor would have to run when you get sick . . . As the saying goes, 'non-toxic' means the mouse did not die, it does not mean the mouse did not have a really bad day or week."

Finally, Stanley has learned to take time for himself. Stanley makes time for acupuncture and Chinese herbal medicine, which he discovered after he shattered his right elbow in a bicycle accident. His acupuncturist, Kenny Gong, taught him the difference between good pain, which is healing, and bad pain or chronic pain. Never underestimate yourself as a designer and the care that you need as well. Take a walk outside to clear your head and enjoy the fresh air. Find a medical practitioner that you trust and can go to. Get a massage. In addition, many young designers are struggling financially or otherwise, as Stanley was when he shattered his arm. When he was struggling, Kenny gave him some sage advice: "People with no money and friends can get anything they need done. People with money and no true friends can lose all their money, and even if they have money they cannot get everything or anything done." Teaching Stanley this lesson, Kenny allowed Stanley to pay for the treatment by restoring a one hundred-year-old Chinese sword covered in stingray skin.

Many times, Stanley's path has taken a turn or gone in an unexpected direction, but for him it is about the adventure itself and figuring out immediate challenges. "Problems are a part of this business," he says, but after listening to his stories I can feel the joy and excitement that he has found and kept for the journey. A journey of a thousand miles that started with a single step: a desire to create and be original.

ARTIST BIO

Stanley Allan Sherman is an early graduate of Ecole Jacques Lecoq in Paris, France, and was present when Philippe Gaulier taught his first class. He has appeared in forty-one comedy bits on NBC's *Late Night With Conan O'Brien* and is a member of the original cast of the Off Broadway hit show *Grandma Sylvia's Funeral* that ran for four years. He was a teacher and mask maker in the late 1970s, working with the master of Commedia dell'arte, Carlo Mazzone-Clementi at Dell'Arte School of Mime and Comedy, also creating Carlo's Metaphysical mask. He has taught mime at Portland State University, clown at Kent State University, and mask making a Hostos CUNY. He has taught many Commedia dell'arte workshops and has cofounded his own school, CommediaU.com. He created the Mankind mask for the World Wrestling Federation, the Queen and Daughter masks for *Queen of the Night* on Broadway, and numerous Commedia dell'arte masks for performers, theatre and dance companies, schools, and universities. Stanley also directs and develops original theatre works with performers. He had the longest-running exhibition in the history of the New York Lincoln Center Museum of the Performing Arts. He is a member of Actors Equity Association, the Screen Actors Guild, and the American Federation of Television and Radio Artists. His mask-making website is www.maskarts.com.

IMAGE 12.8 *Stanley Allan Sherman with the just finished clay sculpture of the Max Headroom mask created for the film* Intrusion, *written and directed by Jesse Lowell Anholt.*

Courtesy of Stanley Allan Sherman.

CHAPTER 13

DENISE WALLACE-SPRIGGS

A Fourth-Generation Craft Artisan

Rachel E. Pollock

IMAGE 13.1 *Denise Wallace-Spriggs.*
Photo by John Ring. Courtesy of Denise Wallace-Spriggs.

For the past thirty years, Denise Wallace-Spriggs has served as the costume crafts artisan for the Huntington Theatre, a LORT-B company based in Boston, Massachusetts. In this capacity, she makes countless incredible costume pieces, from historically accurate millinery to fantastical suits of armor. In addition, she oversees the operation of the Huntington's dye facility, processing custom color requests for yardage, garments, notions, and trimmings. She is also responsible for generating surface design effects using techniques such as screen-printing, batik, and shibori. Her craftwork has been seen on Broadway in productions such as *The 39 Steps*, *Porgy and Bess*, and *Finding Neverland*, and her freelance clients have included Disney Cruise Lines, Big Apple Circus, and Glimmerglass Opera. She is a member of the Surface Design Association, the American Craft Association, and the United States Institute for Theatre Technology.

You've heard of costume designers, sure, and you know that the costume shop staff includes workers with job titles like draper, tailor, cutter, and stitcher, but it's possible that "costume crafts artisan" is an unfamiliar term. You're not alone—not all shops even have them. So what exactly is it that Denise Wallace-Spriggs does? In shops large enough to have production teams, drapers and tailors supervise the creation of actors' clothing with the help of their cutters and stitchers, but every other costume item falls under the purview of the crafts team. Hats, shoes, masks, armor, period accessories like reticules and parasols—the craftsperson handles them all. A crafts artisan is a practitioner of all trades, so to speak, though some large companies or independent costume shops split out specialist positions, such as the Santa Fe Opera, for example, which has a separate millinery team of dedicated artisans who make the hats. At the Huntington Theatre, Denise oversees it all with an impeccable dedication to quality, efficiency, technique, and technology.

THE MAKING OF A MAKER

Denise wasn't born knowing that she wanted to be a costume craftsperson, but she did grow up in a family of makers. "I'm a fourth-generation craft artisan," she states with pride, before listing off examples of the industrial craftsmanship to be found in her family's history—lost-wax casting, pounded-sand casting, even a great-grandfather who carved the wooden positives from which foundry molds are made. Denise sees herself as one more innovative link in a generational creative chain. But when choosing a college major, she didn't consider handcrafts.

As an undergraduate at Bridgewater State College (now University) in Bridgewater, Massachusetts, Denise initially thought she might be a playwright. "I love hearing and telling stories," she admits. In time, when her focus shifted to creative disciplines behind the scenes; she thought instead that perhaps costume design would be where she found artistic fulfillment. "My mentor in undergraduate school took us on a field trip to meet the designer at Rhode Island College, and we hit it off," says Denise. "When she was looking for an assistant, she placed an ad in the paper . . . and I applied. I was her assistant for two years. When I left that job I had no idea what I would do, so I called a local small theatre company and asked if there were any jobs available." The cold call paid off; they did have a position opening and she got her first staff job.

Ultimately, Denise came to embrace craftwork as her place in the costuming field. "I like to make objects with my hands and I like to collaborate to help bring the designer's vision to life. I like to solve problems and get things just right for the performer." That collaborative element is the secret ingredient which sets costume craftwork apart from traditional crafts in which the maker follows their own artistic vision to complete a piece for exhibition or direct sale to a collector.

Although Denise has been on staff at the Huntington for three decades now, she had some impressive early gigs as an assistant to legendary masters in the field. She worked at Michael Curry Designs in Oregon for a brief stint, assisting in the making of giant puppets. Denise enthusiastically admits that she learned a lot from this experience, including something important about her own affinity for scale in craftwork—the pieces created by Michael Curry's workshop are typically quite large, almost like posable scenery. "I don't like to sew on a ladder," she confesses. "I like a project that is lap-sized."

Denise also worked as the assistant milliner under the renowned Janet Linville at the Santa Fe Opera for a summer, back when Denise

IMAGE 13.2 *Millinery from* Sunday in the Park With George *at the Huntington Theatre in Boston, Massachusetts. Actress Jenni Barber and ensemble. Designer: Robert Morgan.*
Photo by Paul Marotta. Courtesy of the Huntington Theatre Creative Commons.

was first starting out as a crafts artisan. Linville would subsequently go on to teach hat-making at the Fashion Institute of Technology in New York City, and she has served as the millinery supervisor at the Metropolitan Opera since 1997. Assisting Linville on the Santa Fe millinery team, Denise learned to trust her own instincts. "The work that we did there gave me a vocabulary for the future," she explains.

With such a diversity of requisite skills, craftspeople learn by doing, more often than not. "Most of my so-called 'training' in costume crafts is from my own explorations," says Denise. The colorant supply company Pro Chemical & Dye regularly offers short workshops on dyestuffs and processes at their facility in Somerset, Massachusetts, one of which Denise attended some years ago. "That set me on my way to learn about the chemistry of dyeing." In the interest of full disclosure, I must mention that, as a crafts artisan myself, Denise was my first mentor in the field; I assisted her at the Huntington on several shows as a freelancer in Boston back in the late 1990s, among my first jobs after getting my BA. I learned many skills and strategies from her that I still use today and impart to my own assistants. Denise taught me tricks of natural skin-tone matching (for a

IMAGE 13.3 *Hat projects from* The Jungle Book, *Huntington Theatre. Akash Chopra (Mowgli) and Kevin Carolan (Baloo) in Tony Award–winner Mary Zimmerman's new musical adaption of* The Jungle Book. *Designer: Mara Blumenfeld.* Photo by Liz Lauren. Courtesy of the Huntington Theatre Creative Commons.

more realistic dye recipe, add just a tiny dash of the color complement to the undertone), and she introduced me to the proper protective equipment for jamming a really huge needle through a thick piece of foam (something called a sailor's palm, which protects the ball of your thumb as you push).

It was Denise who first opened my eyes to the invisible contributions of the craftsperson to the costume designer's vision. The audience may not register why a custom-made hat looks more genuine than a purchased ready-made one, and they may have no idea how dissonant and bright a dress appeared before the dyer "dipped it down," but for those with a discerning eye for detail, the shows of a theatre with a good craftsperson have a sophisticated, unique aesthetic. "In my job as a crafts artisan," Denise explains, "I can help tell the play's story by making the stage picture as honest as possible. If I do my job well, sometimes you won't notice my work at all and that is very satisfying." It's her expertise, skill set, and respectful creative input that make Denise Wallace-Spriggs an integral part of the Huntington's costume department.

COLLABORATION AND RESPECT

Denise has a wonderful approach to the collaborative process in terms of her philosophy for creating in tandem with designers, performers, and costume-makers on her team. Of primary import is her understanding of the crafts artisan's

IMAGE 13.4 *Straw hat with silk trim for* The Corn is Green. *Designer: Robert Morgan.*
Photo by Denise Wallace-Spriggs.

IMAGE 13.5 *Nick Offerman wearing the "Ignatius J. Reilly" body padding for the Huntington Theatre's 2015 production of* A Confederacy of Dunces. *Designer: Michael Krass.*
Photo by Denise Wallace-Spriggs.

role in the hierarchy of creation; Denise brings no egotism to the table and is always mindful of the importance of the costume designer's aesthetic leadership. "I am in a support position," Denise says with pride. "I solve problems and bring a designer's vision to reality." Her ultimate goal for each designer's craftwork is "to give them just what they want and sometimes what they didn't know that they wanted."

A craftsperson's task list sometimes must be approached with a mind to the draper's workflow as well. A highly efficient artisan like Denise is in constant communication with the drapers about their assigned looks and the scheduling of any crafts support, which involves "everything from dyeing and patterning fabrics before the draper cuts them, to distressing the garments after the draper has built them." Denise brings an accommodating professionalism to the fitting process, with mindfulness toward creating a welcoming place for the performer and an accommodating space for the designer. "I try to handle all fittings with the same respect for the person who has entered into the fitting space, which I consider very special," she explains. "The performer is in a vulnerable position, being asked to change clothing and then having the clothing fit on their body while in front of others, while the costume is being discussed." Whether she is working with the greenest student actor or a

IMAGE 13.6 *Nick Offerman wearing the "Ignatius J. Reilly" body padding and costume for the Huntington Theatre's 2015 production of* A Confederacy of Dunces. *Designer: Michael Krass.*
Photo by Charles Erickson. Courtesy of the Huntington Theatre Creative Commons.

celebrity like Nick Offerman (for whom she made the "Ignatius J. Reilly" body padding in the Huntington's 2015 production of *A Confederacy of Dunces*), Denise believes in treating every performer with kindness, and paying careful attention to the nuances of how the costume fitting might affect their concept of their character.

When making a body pad for the renowned actress Phylicia Rashad for a production of August Wilson's *Gem of the Ocean*, Denise knew that the primary point of collaboration in the construction of that garment was with Rashad herself, who would need the padding to accommodate the physically active nature of her character's performance. The fittings for that set of padding resulted in such a successful garment that when Rashad did the play again some months later at another regional theatre, she called the

IMAGE 13.7 *Phylicia Rashad wearing body padding for the Huntington Theatre's production of August Wilson's* Gem of the Ocean. *Also pictured, Anthony Chisholm. Designer: Constanza Romero.*
Photo by T. Charles Erickson. Courtesy of the Huntington Theatre Creative Commons.

Huntington "to ask if she could borrow the body pad, she liked it so much." I hear the grin in Denise's voice as she elaborates, "[Rashad] felt like it was her body when she was playing [Aunt Ester], so I felt like, okay! We did some good work together!"

A TEACHER FOR LIFE

In addition to her production work for professional theatre, Denise has taught graduate-level courses as a component of the Boston University master of fine arts program in costume production and technology for over twenty-five years. She teaches year-long/two-semester courses on millinery and dyeing in alternating years, which provide BU graduates with a comprehensive understanding of both topics, in addition to the education they receive from other faculty in patternmaking, tailoring, and related costume-making topics. Denise's guidance doesn't end with commencement, however. "I have always made it clear to my students that I am their teacher for life," she says, "and I have a mentor relationship with them for many years after they graduate. Sometimes my phone is very busy with text consultations!"

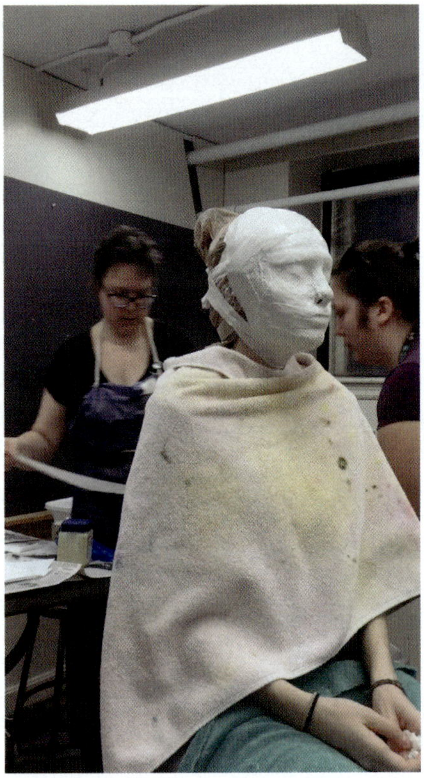

IMAGE 13.8 *Denise Wallace-Spriggs leading a face casting for masks workshop. Casting model: Zarah Avalon. Assistant: Becca Jewett.*
Photo by Denise Wallace-Spriggs.

Millinery is Denise's favorite of all the craftwork disciplines. "I love making every kind of hat from ladies confections to Viking helmets," she says. She begins working with her graduates on a conceptual patterning level, encouraging them to explore three-dimensional hat shapes using paper and cardstock and other inexpensive media. They go on to talk about the geometry of pattern drafting, how to translate three-dimensional shapes to two-dimensional pieces and vice versa, before beginning to work with that time-honored millinery medium, buckram. Only once the grad students are confident in the 2D-to-3D process does she move on to an introduction of other hat-making media and methods: wire structures, blocking in felt and straw, and contemporary thermoformable materials.

If a theatre has space and equipment for dye-work, color control becomes a significant part of the costume production process, and the craftsperson needs the knowledge and skill to fulfill the designers' dye requests. Thus, two semesters of dye topics comprise the other significant coursework in the Boston University graduate-level crafts class offerings. In the first semester, Denise teaches her students about the chemistry of three classes of dyestuffs: fiber-reactive, acid, and direct. She also covers color theory and taxonomies, so that the students have not only a basic understanding of the chemical processes pertaining to the dyes and the applicable fibers, but also gain a solid vocabulary of terms and classification systems (like Pantone) for discussing the finer points of color with a designer or draper/tailor. Once they have mastered the basics, then they get to explore what Denise calls "the fun stuff"—screen-printing, resist techniques, distressing/aging processes, and other surface design elements.

Access to the pedagogical expertise of this experienced artisan is not limited to academics pursuing graduate degrees. Denise regularly offers introductory millinery and dyeing workshops at other colleges and schools in the greater Boston area, as well as classes for "lifelong-learning" students at her studio in Stoughton and through the Eliot School for Fine and Applied Arts in Jamaica Plain (both in Massachusetts). "My father taught me that 'you can't know a thing, until you know a thing,'" she says. "I like to meet students where they are, and work with them on professionalizing their skills. I take great joy from their growth and achievement in my classes and beyond." At the Eliot School, her amateur-level classes are designed for adults interested in millinery. Workshop participants usually have no theatrical or hat-making background. "This situation is very challenging," explains Wallace-Spriggs, "because we all come from different places of experience, and these students do not have a common visual or working vocabulary. By the time we finish, everyone has beautiful hats and new skills."

I asked Denise about how she would compare her pedagogical approach in the context of her Boston University classes for the graduate students to that of her amateur workshop participants. "That's an interesting question," she replied. "It's the difference between training somebody to be a professional and helping someone to develop a love for something." Different students come to the learning process with different goals, and Denise's aim is always to help them achieve those goals, even if failure is one of the steps on the path. "You cannot learn anything of value without some level of failure along the way," she asserts. "Push through the failure because success is on the other side."

What about aspiring craftspeople who want more in-depth study than a weekend workshop, but aren't sure an MFA is the right path either? Denise believes she's got the answer: the culmination of many years' work, she is collaborating with Boston University on a new educational alternative. For the

IMAGE 13.9 *Thomas Derrah (Kaa) and Larry Yando (Shere Khan) in Tony Award–winner Mary Zimmerman's new musical adaption of* The Jungle Book. *Designer: Mara Blumenfeld.*
Photo by Liz Lauren. Courtesy of the Huntington Theatre Creative Commons.

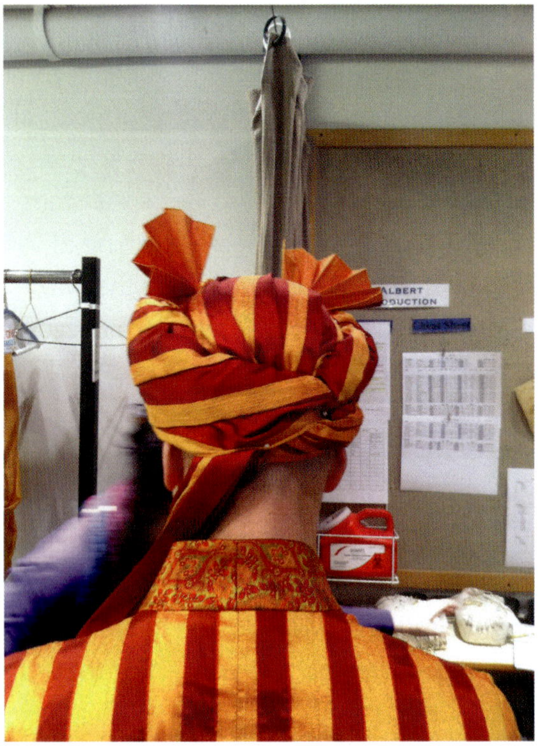

IMAGE 13.10 *Back detail of Kaa's headpiece for Tony Award–winner Mary Zimmerman's new musical adaption of* The Jungle Book. *Designer: Mara Blumenfeld.*
Photo by Denise Wallace-Spriggs.

past fifteen years, Boston University has administered a unique certification credential in the technical theatre arts. The Professional Certificate Program is designed to augment an undergraduate degree with coursework in a specific focus for a student interested in going into a backstage profession but who does not feel that a graduate degree will best serve their goals. Diane Fargo's scenic painting certificate program has flourished since its inception, and in the intervening time, Boston University has added focus concentrations in stage management, technical production, and props.

Denise is in the process of launching a new curriculum in costume crafts; in addition to millinery and dyeing, she plans to add classes in theatrical body padding, working with leather, mask making, period accessories, and theatrical armor making for a comprehensive course of study in costume craft technology through the credential program. Perhaps by the time of this book's printing, the new concentration will be accepting applications for candidates.

I asked Denise her advice for aspiring young craftspeople in the meantime. "Keep trying new things," she recommends. "Seek out critique and mentorship from people that you trust and admire, and listen to it." The dye chemistry workshop Denise took through Pro Chemical & Dye is only one example of the kind of topical learning opportunities an early career craftsperson might employ to improve their skillset. Weekend workshops in millinery are hosted all over the country by fashion milliners and through institutions like FIT and Judith M Millinery Supply. Corporations like Smooth-On, Wonderflex World, and Reynolds Advanced Materials offer seminars in working with their products, and USITT's annual costume symposium provides a long weekend's focus on a different topic each year; past craft-centric symposia have featured mascot construction methods, wig making, and surface design techniques. Denise also encourages her students, crafts assistants, and colleagues to consider teamwork their paramount skill to cultivate for success. In theatre, no one succeeds alone. "I like to think of what I do as 'group art,'" she says. "We work together to bring the playwright's ideas to fruition. Sometimes, when the pressure of a deadline is on, and you are humming along at top speed with a group of committed artisans who have each other's best interests at heart, that is the most fun you can have at work."

INNOVATION AND THE FUTURE OF MAKING COSTUMES

In over thirty years, Denise has seen a lot of progress in the means and methods of theatrical costume production, from the development of digitally driven technologies to a sea change in the industry's attitudes toward work safety. "I have tools and materials to work with now," she explains, "that I could have only dreamed of at the beginning."

For example, back in the late 1990s Denise was one of the first theatrical craftspeople to experiment with the then-new thermoplastic materials we now know as Fosshape and Wonderflex. Prior to their development (initially for industrial use in the shoemaking industry), craftspeople were limited to traditional foundation materials like buckram, felt, papier maché, and millinery willow (the manufacture of which had been discontinued in the mid-twentieth century), or the acetone-activated Celastic. Because thermoplastics are heat activated instead of solvent activated, Fosshape and Wonderflex not only allow the craftsperson to work quicker in the production of a costume piece, but they also don't require the protective gear and safety precautions of a medium like Celastic.

In 2004, in tandem with Liz Perlman of Boston's Costume Works (a commercial shop known for its contracts with Broadway and regional theatres, theme parks, touring entertainment, and corporate clients), Denise initially used Fosshape thermosformable felt

IMAGE 13.11 *Assembly of Dot's hat from* Sunday in the Park With George *at the Huntington Theatre. Designer: Robert Morgan.*
Photo by Denise Wallace-Spriggs.

IMAGE 13.12 *A pack of wolf ears made of Fosshape covered with brocade for* The Jungle Book. *Designer: Mara Blumenfeld.*
Photo by Denise Wallace-Spriggs.

IMAGE 13.13 *Headpiece for the Big Apple Circus. Designer: Sarah Connelly.*
Photo by Denise Wallace-Spriggs.

in the remaking of Julie Taymor's millinery designs for the American Repertory Theatre's twentieth-anniversary *King Stag* revival at Harvard University. The uniquely appealing properties of the material were immediately apparent to Denise and Liz both, and now it has become as commonly used in craft shops as buckram ever was.

The general trend in innovation seems to be toward not only higher-efficiency media and methods, but also toward safer products and equipment. The strides that have been made in manufacturing non- and less-toxic materials have lowered health risk factors in the crafts artisan's work on the whole. Denise is not alone among experienced craftspeople in saying, "I blush to think of the unsafe practices that were in use when I was coming up." Everyone has a story about a craftsperson of a prior generation who developed nerve damage from overexposure to methylated solvents, or a dyer who passed away from respiratory disease. Thanks to the efforts of industrial health and safety expert Monona Rossol of the Arts, Crafts, and Theatre Safety (ACTS) Network and well-informed craftspeople like Denise Wallace-Spriggs, the culture of technical theatre is changing for the better. They work hard to educate colleagues, assistants, and students in the field about safe work practices and protective equipment (like fit-tested respirators, product-appropriate gloves, safety goggles, and so forth).

New products, processes, and equipment have definitely increased the speed of production. "Things need to be and can be done so much faster now," explains Denise. "When I began my career [at the Huntington], we were doing five shows in a season; now we do nine or ten. This has partly been made possible by computers. Computers have allowed for faster delivery of information and supplies and have sped up sharing from one theatre to another. In the 'olden days,' if you wanted to rent stock from another theatre, you would have to send a photocopy packet via the US Mail to the other theatre and would have to wait . . . for a giant box of costumes to arrive [via parcel post]. This is no longer the case. Another thing that has changed is the access to accurate period costume research via the Internet. I used to spend hours in the public library, hoping that there would be a helpful book in the collection; now it is at my fingertips." Pinterest on a smartphone has replaced the pasted-up collage of research imagery in record time.

Not only have computers enhanced the speed of communication and research, but they've opened whole new areas of digitally driven manufacturing. For example, over the last decade, the increased availability, affordability, and quality of digitally printed textiles have expanded the custom-printed options for costume designers. With advance planning, complex repeats can be created in image-editing software like Photoshop, Illustrator, GIMP, or InkScape and printed on a wide range of different textiles.

Of course, that doesn't mean the labor of the dyer/painter is no longer needed. Some designers are unfamiliar with the process of creating the digital artwork files in the format commercial printers require, and sometimes the printed fabric when it arrives is not quite what the designer wanted. Theatre productions have their hard deadline of opening night, and if a custom-printed textile arrives but the colors don't work well under the lights or the print

IMAGE 13.14 *The inside of hats for* Sunday in the Park With George. *Designer: Robert Morgan.* Photo by Denise Wallace-Spriggs.

contains an unexpected registration error, it falls to the crafts artisan to strategize a way to fix the issue. About a hypothetical digitally printed polyester textile, Denise speculates, "I can't dip it in the dye because it's not going to take . . . so [I'm] spraying it all down or something like that. You have to think quickly." The source of the printed fabric may be innovative, but often the solution for making it stage worthy involves the same creative thinking that craftspeople have always explored.

The same vector file that a craftsperson or costume designer uploads for digitally printed fabric can now be used for a whole host of other CDC ("computer-driven control") equipment. Digital embroidery machines can stitch the designs onto fabric, and laser cutters/etchers can put it onto acrylic, wood, leather, and more. Now an artisan can take a 3D scan of something—a mask, a medallion, a parasol handle—and 3D print a copy of it using any number of different filaments. The designer has a set of Deco dress clips . . . but one's damaged and really, they ought to be 25% larger? Scan one, digitally resize it, and print two at the desired bigger scale. This is the current cusp of innovation and change in the field of crafts, and while Denise herself isn't directly involved with 3D fabrication yet with respect to Huntington craftwork, she encourages and guides her graduate students whose scholarly interests or thesis topics take them in that direction. And if fabrication turns out to be the Fosshape of the twenty-first

IMAGE 13.15 *Denise Wallace-Spriggs at her studio.*
Photo by John Ring.

century, Denise will gladly avail herself of yet another new set of tools.

In this field, we're always asked why the theatre is the place where we choose to practice our craft. Why not give it up to make hats for the fashion industry, for example? So I asked Denise what she thought about the why of the matter. "I can't think of any subject or topic or culture that doesn't cross the stage at some point," she said. "History, philosophy, art, storytelling, mathematics . . . every single thing that you can think of comes to the stage, so why go anywhere else? It's all gonna be there."

ARTIST BIO

Denise Wallace-Spriggs has an MFA in costume production and technology from Boston University, where she has taught millinery, dyeing, and costume crafts for twenty-five years. She is currently the resident crafts artisan/dyer for the Huntington Theatre Company in Boston, which won the regional Tony Award in 2013. She is also the proprietor of Winged Heart Millinery, where she makes custom hats. Denise also does freelance millinery and crafts for clients such as the Manhattan Theatre Club, Disney Cruise Line, Big Apple Circus, American Repertory Theater, and the Glimmerglass Opera. In addition to theatre and opera work, Denise does freelance dyeing and millinery for films in the New England area and teaches freelance workshops in millinery and dyeing at local colleges. Her professional design experience includes three years as the resident designer at the Wellesley College Theatre Department and freelance costume design in the Boston area. She is the 2015 recipient of the Dr. Adrian Tinsley Award for Achievement in the Arts from her alma mater, Bridgewater State University. Visit her website at https://denisewallacespriggs.com/. You can also see the Arts, Crafts, & Theatre Safety site at www.artscraftstheatersafety.org and the La Bricoleuse craft artisanship blog at https://la-bricoleuse.blogspot.com/.

CHAPTER 14

KNOW THE VALUE OF YOUR IDEAS

An Interview With Michael Curry[1]

Skye Strauss

IMAGE 14.1 *Michael Curry at work in his Portland, Oregon, studio.*
Courtesy of Michael Curry Design.

Michael Curry's office sits on the "clean" side of his complex outside Portland, Oregon. A window over his executive-style desk faces the Sauvie Island Wildlife Area. Via FaceTime you can see the cloudy afternoon sky stretching out over the parking lot to the tree line beyond. Meanwhile, I am sitting in the lakeside offices of Northwestern University where the sun has already set. Curry admits it is a blessing of the digital age to work so close to the wilderness: "I don't think twenty years ago I could have come to a rural area and [remained] connected to the world stage . . . but because, really, we're working in Europe, Asia, [and] the U.S. eventually I find that it matters less where you're at." His international reputation is backed by multiple awards; highlights include two Drama Desk Awards for Outstanding Puppet Design for Disney's *Frozen* and *The Lion King*, a Risorgimento Creativity Award for "lifelong creativity and risk taking in the fields of technical and artistic design," and two Emmy Awards for his work on the Olympic Opening Ceremonies and a third for Best Masks, Costumes, and Body Sculpture for the televised opera *Oedipus Rex*. The facility for Michael Curry Design encompasses three buildings over sixty-five thousand square feet that were "designed specifically for what we do" by the man himself. Curry estimates the average employee has been with the company for ten years. He credits the retention rate to the improved quality of life in this location compared to the "revolving door" in his former New York workshop. Longevity allows him to "rely on a knowledgeable core group of consistent collaborators." His journey from studio artist to award-winning theatrical designer and company manager has been driven by a constant pursuit of both excellence and equity, honoring the stories that he tells while carving out space for his own artistic vision.

On the other side of his desk the windows look down on the "dirty" part of the busy workshop. Curry offers me an impromptu digital tour of the studio. On the way downstairs, he passes a conference table and wall-sized image boards set up for client presentations. The computer-generated stills showcase the variety of work moving through the shop, including ninja black jet skis pulling LED kites, large-scale robots, and multistory boots for a pop-star extraordinaire. We soon reach the work benches where the designs cross over into reality. He picks up the unpainted form of what appears to be a roast pig. He demonstrates how it rears up and gyrates on its serving tray platform. Familiar characters from cartoon feature films are also present in various stages of assembly. But Curry stresses that even before the finishing work they are anything but incomplete in his eyes, because he is in love with the structure, the mechanics, and the problem-solving each one represents.

Curry happily talks me through construction details to point out the technology that makes the shop tick. That full-scale Volkswagen Beetle? It belongs to *The Beatles Love* by Cirque du Soleil at the Mirage in Las Vegas. Technicians molded it from carbon fiber mesh so it clocks in at only thirty-two pounds despite its size. It will be effortless to carry distributed over a team of twelve dancers. Passing into the engineering offices, he points out a cadre of 3D printers that are "going nearly all the time." One faithfully reproduces a character from a Disney film in mounting layers of molten plastic, giving it a new dimensional life. While the printers can replicate familiar characters from their corporate models, it is important that the scanners in the adjacent room can map *anything*. A recent application included copying the face of the lead dancer for the Oregon Symphony Orchestra's production of Stravinsky's *Persephone*. Her uncanny puppet double and masked counterparts mirrored her exactly despite their differences in scale. Small models testing mechanical concepts litter the nearby desks, including a jointed tail for the dinosaur currently being incubated in the scanner. The nearby costume department seems less high tech, but Curry clarifies: "We use fabric to make things large and flexible, the movement of fabric is still one of our main tools." Finally, he explains that the unseen buildings across the street host a fully equipped stage and an industrial mold-making facility. The team has the means to build anything they can dream.

The unusual location of the workshop marks an intentional homecoming for Curry, who "was raised in a faith healing branch of the Christian religion in southern Oregon" before embarking on his artistic career. "The earliest sort of theatrical things" he was exposed to were church services where congregants played music, spoke in tongues, and baptized in the river. That changed "when I was twelve years old in 1970, hippies from southern California and San Francisco started moving into our valley and opening communes. My first sculpture lesson was from an old man who made wax candles," which was swiftly followed by guitar lessons, impromptu dance performances, and a newfound love of drawing. Curry explains: "I carried a sketchbook like a young Van Gogh . . . I started drawing constantly, and I thought that this held some thread to my future." Following that path would require deviating from the norm. Growing up in that community, "chances were I was going to be working in the logging industry in Oregon." Another shift challenged that assumption when "the Sierra Club petitioned that the spotted owl be protected in southern Oregon, and so all the logging was stopped by a federal mandate . . . the promise of my easy transition into being a blue-collar forest worker suddenly wasn't an option. So thank god we had a recession, 'cause this kid chose to dive into something unexpected."

The next step came when the ceramics teacher at his high school took notice of his talent. She began sending sketches to art schools to assess his talent and help him acquire necessary funding. He secured "a scholarship in 1976 to go to what was called the Museum Art School; it was an adjunct program of the Portland Art Museum." He recalls that the transition was shocking as he "went from a faith-healing commune to, in 1976, the pinnacle of the Vietnam War vets returning and the first stages of feminism." Prior to freshman year he "had never met a black person, a gay person, anything—and I was so stunted by that. Fortunately for me a lot of the professors at the school recognized that." He was given leave from the program with "marching orders of what to study to refine myself." After taking a year to adjust, he recalls, "I came back a much better student in 1978 when I returned, and then ended up being their big success story." After graduation he moved to New York where he acquired a studio, found a gallery willing to exhibit his work, and began establishing himself in the fine arts as a painter and sculptor.

Curry admits that his style was out of fashion: "I went to art school in the middle of abstract expressionism, but I wanted to paint narrative representational things . . . like Norman Rockwell at the time of Jackson Pollock." He realized the content brought clarity to his process because "it's easier for me to commit to an idea or color or shape when I know the story behind it." The Greenwich Village Halloween Parade turned out to be the perfect outlet. The first time he attended he was struck by how "pagan and fun" it was compared to the gallery. He began work on a pterodactyl costume "seven months early and the piece grew bigger and more complicated." His excitement is still palpable as he recalls its debut: "The first night I wore my pterodactyl costume for thirteen hours *and it weighed eight-five pounds*." The experience transformed his practice. Creatively and professionally, it "really was as pivotal as anything that's ever happened to me." At the party, John Napier gave him a business card, which led to his first performing arts contract for an upcoming Siegfried and Roy show. This was followed by costume and costume crafts contracts with Parsons-Meares, LTD and designer William Ivey Long.

The shift from costumes to puppetry, or what Curry calls "sculptural costumes" due to the centrality of the human body, took longer to evolve. "I really liked the idea of moving sculpture, so I drafted for a whole year." He had not been given the right opportunities yet, but he says, "I had some ideas that were what I would *like* to do" that found form on paper. He is pleasantly surprised looking back on those early blueprints with "thirty years of technical skill" to see that they "still hold up pretty well." Contrary to the usual wisdom, Curry started showing these unrealized projects to high-level directors looking for the right fit between concept and project. These encounters taught him to have conviction about presenting his ideas to potential clients. Curry calls that kind of negotiation a "[h]uge skill that all artists should work on . . . convincing people of the value of *your* idea." That persistence has allowed him to realize his ideas in partnership with his clients instead of leaving innovative concepts unrealized on the sidelines. Those early human–animal hybrids mark the beginning of a trend that flows through his work to the present day.

Curry's negotiation skills sell his best ideas instead of waiting for an ideal contract. Sometimes this means investing in staging his own work. Self-financed "showcase" pieces have allowed him to "try out some ideas that my commercial clients were less apt to let me do." For the Michael Curry Design showcase *Spirits*, a puppetry and dance piece that premiered in 2001, Curry pursued a long-standing interest in the supernatural by compiling research on "archetypal characters that come up in completely unrelated societies" that were distilled into "a series of vignettes only held together by this idea of a spirit medium who is sort of journeying through the world of spirits." Curry's favorite character for the production was "a standing frontal figure made out of bodies" that represented the act of possession, with many spirits inhabiting a single, mortal frame. These showcases energize subsequent contract work; for instance, "the break apart Volkswagen in *Love* the Cirque du Soleil [show] came from a direct experiment I did in *Spirits*." Curry admits that he "spent maybe half a million dollars of studio money to put that up" but in return "what it did was get a lot of people who were on the fence about using my services to say, 'Whoa! This guy's riskier than I thought.' And that was my introduction to a few clients including Cirque du Soleil . . . I negotiated with them a couple of weeks later to do *Kà*."

Kà by Cirque du Soleil, directed by Robert Lepage, had unprecedented resources during its development. Curry specifies that the team "had two and a half years" and spent hundreds of millions of dollars creating the show, and virtually "nobody does that anymore." Whatever the team imagined, they could pursue, including video screen platforms rigged for climbing, explosive fire effects, and the "wheel of death" apparatus for the spectacular final battle. One of the contraptions that fell under his purview as puppeteer was a bird that provides the story's heroes with a mode of escape. He clarifies "that [the] beast was conceived by the late-great Mark Fisher" and that the whole creative team helped to storyboard the sequence where "the skins of the teepee itself would become the bird." It was important to mask the puppet's internal sophistication so that it fit into the rough-hewn world of the production; "it looks like animal skins, but it's a titanium frame with specialized Dacron fabric that's been treated to look like leather and little tufts of synthetic hair sewn around the edges." As the performers prepare for their flight over the house "it's like a quick-change costume, you brace yourself in—there's two or three redundant forms of attachment, there always has to be with anything that's over the audience—and *then* the piece becomes very graceful and light. But it's really a complex piece of engineering. I always liked that scene." You sense that he relishes the challenge of making fantasy into reality.

Curry wholeheartedly believes that collaborative problem-solving, like the work done on the flying bird, is an important part

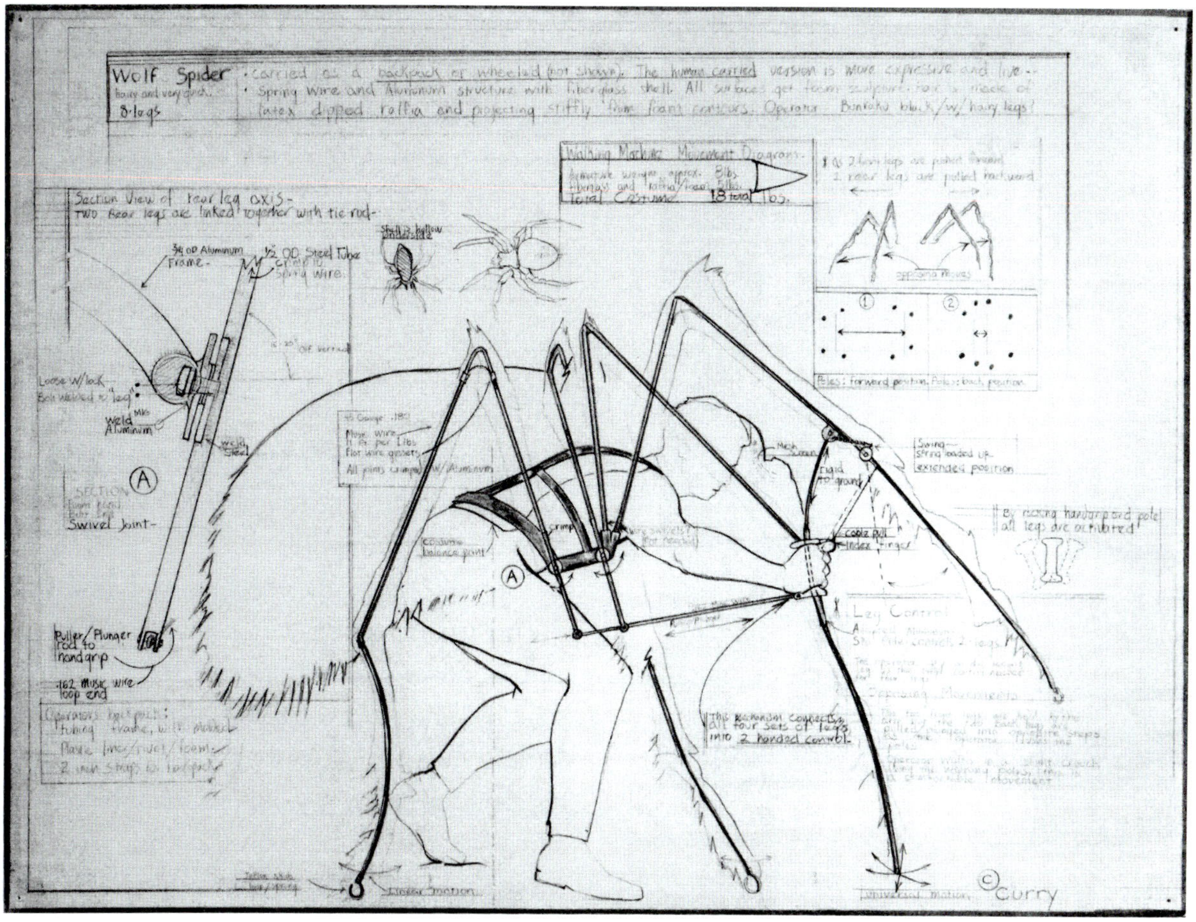

IMAGE 14.2 *Concept blueprint for a puppeteer-operated wolf spider.*
Courtesy of Michael Curry Design.

of a healthy design process. "When it works best" bringing a production to the stage is "really a blending of ideas." However, he clarifies that he still adheres to "the sort of pyramid structure" governed by a visionary director who can protect the coherence of the production. Without it, "people get so ego driven that they *thrust* something upon a story that may be successful in their own artistic vision, but it may not connect to a broad idea." He stresses that as a designer "you're really trying to be a storyteller." This also means listening carefully to clients. Curry recalls an early mishap when he "designed a very expensive, beautiful golden tree for a Chinese project. I used a weeping willow because they're gorgeous forms." The project had progressed through renderings and a model before going into a client meeting. On arrival, "everybody was sort of dumbfounded" because "I overlooked that the willow tree connotes death, and I was putting it in this very lively resort casino." Returning to the proverbial drawing board, Curry "quickly changed it to a golden *oak* tree" which "represents the wealth of the emperor, and people were very astounded that my client understood the

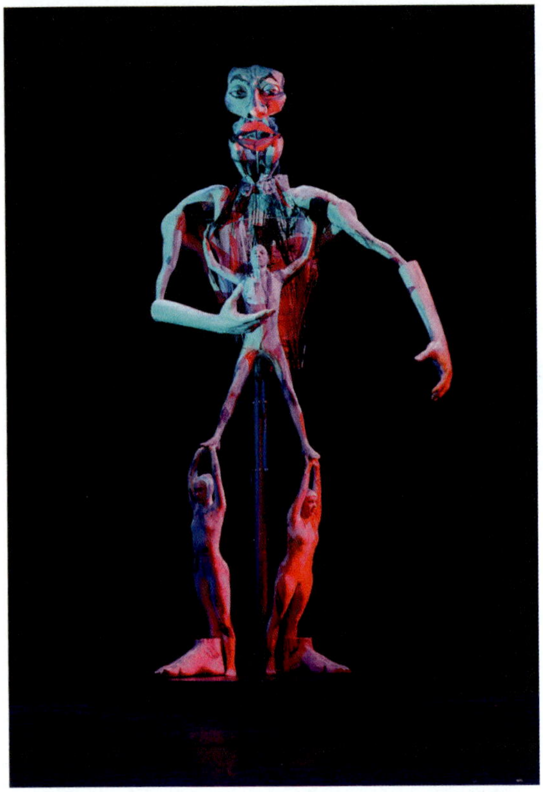

IMAGE 14.3 *Three puppeteers operate the body of "The Medium" in* Spirits.
Courtesy of Michael Curry Design.

connection to the Chinese culture in such a significant way." After that "very expensive mistake," the company now consults "cultural advisors as much as possible."

Raw materials play an important role in the creative process as projects progress from concept to realized design. He explains that as a maker, "[a] material can give you the possibility of a form that you never considered artistically, and so there's a really beautiful dance between the touching and experimenting with materials and the sort of energy they provide you in terms of possibilities." He introduces new products to the team in "what we call R&D" (research and development). The shop begins by using the components according to the manufacturer's guidelines and then branches out into other unexpected applications. When company representatives visit the facility "[t]hey're kind of shocked" at how things have been repurposed "because elastomeric resin that's meant to coat a gym floor would be used to cast an eyeball for an elephant or something." Often the companies are subsequently willing to provide them with product for free to be privy to the results. In those partnerships, "you get the benefit of their experience and they win because suddenly the day is not so boring, you know—they get to make an elephant eye instead of a gym floor."

Some supplies stick around even in the face of constant invention. While Curry avidly tracks innovations in material science, some of his standbys are "very old fashioned things" like the same "rabbit skin glue" that "Leonardo primed his canvasses with." He admits that he has an affinity for real leather because it "survives all these side-by-side comparative tests with lots of different materials. It's elegant in elasticity, shock absorption, [and] its ability to create an aesthetic cover." Returning to the team's experiments with elephants, he talks about a photo-realistic puppet the team created for a German pop star that was covered with "seventy pig skins that we specially treated with a hot knife to create all the wrinkles of an elephant." He credits one of his "twenty-year employees" with inventing the process for texturing the bulk-bought animal skins. She discovered that pressing the leather into a foam crevice with a heat tool "creates an indentation, a deep ridge that stays there forever, and it's dark 'cause it's burnt the leather. So you already have the perfect rendering of the darkness of the fold of the pig skin." The final effect is truly striking.

Curry jokes about subscribing to the trade magazine *Plastics Today*. It may not sound thrilling, but Curry says that staying abreast of material innovations makes his art better. He is "especially drawn to things that are lightweight because gravity is the biggest challenge. By being lighter we control the movement better and then the actors can actually handle the bigger forms that we use in our sculptures." For instance, the transition from fiberglass to carbon fiber facilitated the realization of *The Lion King*, directed by Julie Taymor, twenty-two years ago when "that was the first show that anybody ever used that on." Fiberglass "used to be state of the art, and toxic, and people hated working with it." It was replaced by composite carbon fiber fabric combined with an epoxy resin that is "60 percent lighter than fiberglass and it's much stronger." He admits that it is more expensive, but it revolutionized the size range of wearable pieces. That adaptability and cutting-edge technology has led to repeat collaborations. Curry explains that his partnership with Taymor has always been a joy: "What a great pleasure for a high-concept artist like Julie to be able to just blue sky an idea" knowing someone can make it a reality. Curry proudly explains "that's what I do for her" as her co-designer and technical executor.

Working with familiar characters means negotiating between audience expectations and the desire to envision something new. For Curry, there is a distinct gap between theme park work and the license that comes with a Broadway production where the work is expected to take on a new level of sophistication. When working with feature animation in a parks environment, he always begins with "what's called 'on-model' references." Yet those cartoons were never made with a human body in mind. The challenge lies in trying to "change them *only as much as I have to* to make them useable on stage . . . I'm a translator there, an *interpreter* as much as I'm anything." Curry insists that both kinds of work, the faithful and the flexible, are important because for many audience members it is the "first time they'll ever see theatre. So I actually feel that it's a fairly noble cause to try to do it as good as can be done, because you might be creating, you know, a theatre lover. And we have had letters forwarded to us by families that write to Disney and say, 'I didn't know that it would change my life seeing this show' and they're very kind about sending those on to the creators" of the live-action productions.

Curry is careful to control the amount of external influences that affect his creative process when he has greater artistic license. Before combing the library or the Internet, "I research my subconscious. I don't look at my portfolio, I look at what the signals" from the script or the music "are telling me." He advises that "one of the worst things you can do as a young artist . . . is research how all the most established artists that you look up to handle the same subject." Curry finds that approach "completely debilitating" because he is "so infected by the strength of that work." Real success comes from taking risks rather than being a follower and "[y]ou feel much better about the result when it is personal to you." That influences the way the Michael Curry Design team conducts "design sessions." he explains, "I often don't tell people what they're going to work on," and they surrender their cell phones on the way in. The team listens to the incoming material as a collective and brainstorms about colors, textures, and forms "and then we write down a list of things from that group." Those thoughts routinely

IMAGE 14.4 *Photo-realistic elephant puppet in the workshop.*
Courtesy of Michael Curry Design.

prove "pretty accurate to the substance of what the piece is." Curry encourages artists approaching a new idea to "give it *one minute*" of uninterrupted silence to "let the signals come out from inside" and then without hesitation "put down something on the page" so that your unique thoughts are woven into the work.

When I asked Curry if he could predict the way a character would be grafted onto a human body from paper alone, he insisted that live experiment is still an irreplaceable part of the process. For instance, he says, "I'm looking at you as a polar bear," asking me to imagine inhabiting one of his famous human–animal hybrids. "I'd first direct some motion and then" as you lumbered around the studio "I'd start taping some cardboard to you." In this way, ideas quickly spring from the paper into three dimensions. Curry explains that "[a]lmost everything we do here intersects a movement test, a couple times a day [so] it is really important that I'm close to the builders," so he makes rounds "like a surgeon who gets to see the patient every morning for a set amount of time." He explains that the movement suffers when designers outsource their fabrication because "[y]ou have to touch and feel your way through things . . . There's puppetry that looks good, and there's puppetry that looks *and moves well*, and to combine those things effectively requires a big commitment from the designer" to constantly check the functional properties of the puppet as well as its aesthetic appearance. The standing desks throughout the shop facilitate the necessary active experimentation by making sure "we're always ready to be that polar bear" at a moment's notice.

Achieving successful person–puppet symbiosis also means protecting the human body within the puppet. Curry jokes, "[i]f you don't know the human body and ergonomics you wouldn't be a better puppet designer than you would a furniture designer." He advises that all would-be puppeteers "study the mechanics of the human body, it will it makes your pieces more effective because they'll be more performable." Sometimes that means adapting a concept to accommodate different bodies. For instance, the crab in *Kà* was redesigned in 2009 to accommodate a forward-bending contortionist "because we were having difficulty getting the level of contortionist we needed to do the back bend to make the [original] crab walk." Over time, that need to protect the performer translated into a series of objective standards: "you can't carry more than 25 percent of your body weight, and it has to be distributed 60 percent on your hips 40 percent on your shoulders, and the human head can't have more than 2.3 pounds on it." Making creations wearable allows the performer to use the puppet as an extension of self. Curry explains, "I find the most vital parts of my career were really about getting actors and dancers to expand their range, and not [about] sculpture" confined within gallery walls.

For Curry, the best puppetry fulfills a specific dramaturgical purpose. He explains that the animation of the inanimate "makes people *look* harder and *listen* more carefully." However, he says "[i]f a human can express it entirely with their own craft, I stop there" because puppetry is most effective when the story transcends the potential of the human body. Curry recalls, "[w]hen special effects first started happening in film I could see a direct correlation to more and more effects being asked for onstage" that opened the door to puppetry. Supporting the puppet's narrative function also means integrating stylistically it into the world of the production. Consequently, he strives to be a "bit of a chameleon" and credits his company's success to their flexibility: "Looking back at my thirty years it is pretty awesome how many different styles we've worked in. We change our technique to better match the narrative." For instance, their current work on a musical with a horror-movie aesthetic "can't be beautiful and symmetrical, it has to be hand-crafted" so it spends more time in with individual artisans. The robots and cars necessitate a different machine-polished finished, so they are created with more industrial mold-making techniques that give an industrial finish across multiple copies. The team is forever adapting their methods to the work at hand.

Curry's advice for young artists arises from his own experience. He admits that being a working artist is difficult: "I don't know why people go into the arts. It must truly be a vocation that you cannot avoid." You can test your resolve by reaching out to industry professionals to find out what their careers are really like and allow them to assess your potential. Practical experience and classroom learning serve radically different functions. He stresses that the value of a university education is more about communication and work ethic than acquiring a skill set. He prioritizes direct contact with the industry because "[y]ou can pay for refinement by going to college and going into all the debt, but you can also have a great, vibrant, *free* education alongside side that just being out there in the scene." Curry "decided being shy had no place in the ladder of success" early in his career. Because he was bold enough to ask, entertainment industry greats like Siegfried Fischbacher of Siegfried and Roy and lighting designer Jules Fisher were willing to offer their advice. Curry suggests that young artists be prepared because "you have to give them something too." In his case, "I did plenty of assisting for free" because "you can't just bother them, you have to be interesting to them." You can then "learn from practice, be paid to learn" through internships, jobs, or industry contacts, because techniques are constantly evolving and may outstrip what is being taught within the academy.

Curry is conscious of passing on his accumulated knowledge to younger designers and makers: "I'm sixty next month so I realize that yeah, I've accomplished a lot, there's no reason to be selfish about this." That starts with his shop culture where he focuses on finding teachable moments to share with staff, "I'm constantly out there prophesizing about visual elements that people overlook" like extolling the virtues of a particular shade of blue. As a result, working with the company becomes an education unto itself. He points out that "there are Michael Curry Design veterans who have moved on and are doing quite well in the world, many of them are working on my shows with me. Nicholas [Mahon] is assisting me on three shows this year" after completing puppets for the 2018 Winter Olympic Games. Curry's winding path into the arts has also fostered

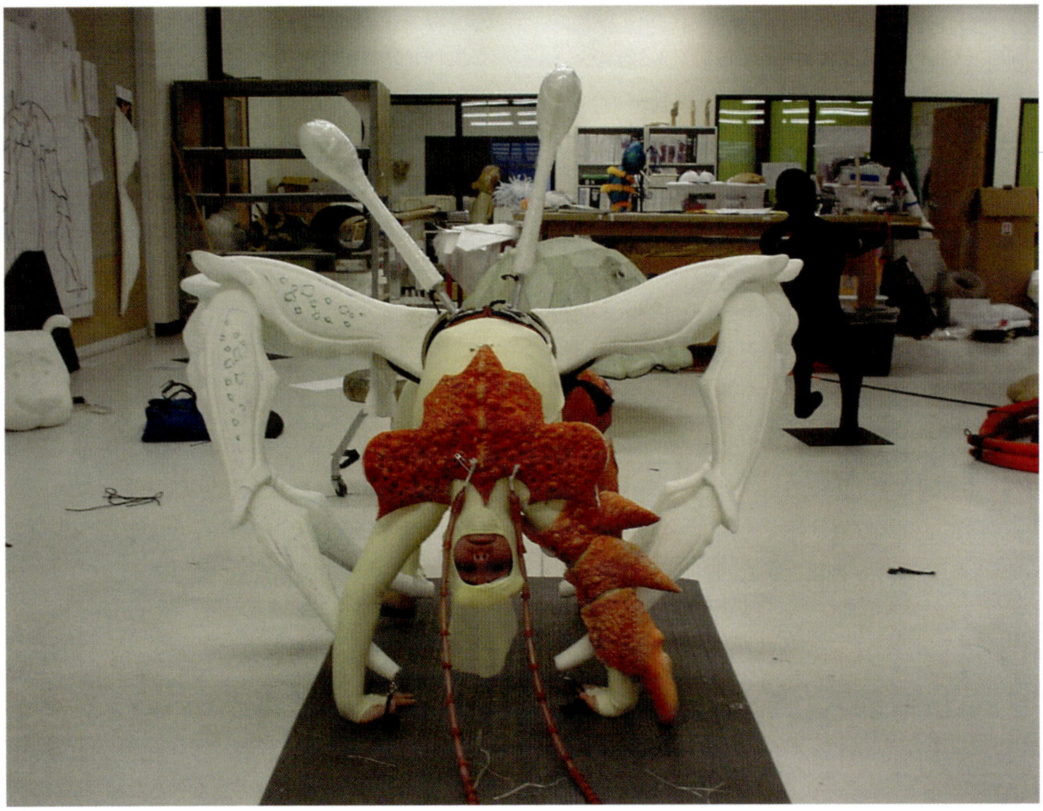

IMAGE 14.5 *The original crab from Kà, operated by a backwards bending contortionist.* Courtesy of Michael Curry Design.

a connection with community members. The studio hosts workshops aimed at "exposing people who are not the likely candidates to be cultural" to the arts so "[t]hey can make their own choice." The company does "a lot of things with schools. Usually vocational training classes—whether it be woodworking from a high school class or a sewing class from a local college." Curry believes arts education is important because "we would be much better environmentally, and a more sound community, if we understood the implications of making for yourself . . . The 'maker's revolution' is very much present out here" in Oregon.

Closing the conversation, I asked where readers should watch for Michael Curry's upcoming work. His previous commercial success allows him to "experiment a little more" with smaller, less economically driven projects "and I'm hoping the next decade of my career will be even freer." However, "small" for Michael Curry is certainly relative since he has no shortage of top-shelf creative partners. For instance, he will be making puppets for the forthcoming *The Beast in the Jungle* at the Vineyard Theater, which is a new musical by John Kander (composer of *Chicago* and *Cabaret*). Curry takes stock mid-sentence and concludes "there's about eighteen Tony Awards among our collaborators," including director Susan Stroman. His work as the co-designer for *The Lion King* contributed to a production that won six Tony Awards. It seems that the scale of the venue defines the project as "small" since it will premiere in "a tiny little one-hundred-thirty–seat theatre" and "it's only running for three months in New York." Michael Curry Design has also begun focusing on finding new venues. "I'm very keen on getting my work presented in other areas besides a black-box theatre. So I've been very interested in interactive work, things in the public sphere . . . I've been doing urban and architectural design," including interactive museum spaces. The company is also beginning to "work for festivals like the Electric Daisy Carnival," an annual event with spectacular lighting displays in Las Vegas, "because it's a new audience." Curry proudly adds that he has "a daughter who's a comedy writer and a son who's an electronic music composer," so he looks forward to "collaborating with them in the near future." His company and the breadth of his creative work will continue to expand for many years to come.

ARTIST BIO

Michael Curry's international career as a production designer, puppet designer, and costuming and character designer spans thirty years. Collaborators include some of the world's most renowned entertainment companies, such as The Walt Disney Company, Cirque du Soleil, the Olympic Committee, the Super Bowl 2012 Halftime Show, the 2011 Pan Am Games, and the Metropolitan Opera. Concerts and tours include Miley Cyrus, Katy Perry's 2014 Prismatic Tour, Lady Gaga, Cher's Farewell Tour, and Britney Spears's 2011 Femme Fatale Tour. Stage productions include the Oregon Symphony's *Persephone*, the opera *Oedipus Rex*, *The Lion King* on Broadway, and *Shrek the Musical*. You can learn more about Michael Curry Design at www.michaelcurrydesign.com.

NOTE

1. This piece is a compilation of three interviews between Michael Curry and Skye Strauss conducted in the winter and spring of 2018.

BIOGRAPHIES

EDITORS AND MENTORS

Rafael Jaen, Main Editor

Jaen (pronounced HA-EN) is a professional costume designer, professor, and author. His design work for film, TV, and theatre has received multiple accolades. He is the recipient of the Kennedy Center Golden Medallion for Excellence in Theatre Education, the Life Achievement in the Arts Award (2016) by the Center for Creative and Performing Arts at Salem State University, and the Manning Prize for Excellence in Teaching 2017 at UMass Boston. He is also the recipient of a Joseph P. Healey Research Grant (2014–2015) titled "Secession, Entrepreneurship and Haute Couture in the USA During the Civil War Years." Jaen made "The Most Stylish Bostonians" list in 2014, and his designs are featured in the *Costume Design at the Turn of the Century 1990–2015* exhibit. He is an elected Board Director of the United States Institute for Theatre Technology (USITT) and the Vice-President for Communications. He is the author of *Show Case* (FOCAL Press) and *Digital Costume Design and Collaboration* (FOCAL Press/Routledge). Additionally, he co-wrote two chapters for the book *Fashioning Horror: Dressing to Kill on Screen and Literature* (Bloomsbury). Website: www.rafael.jaen.biz.

Holly Poe Durbin, Second Editor

Poe Durbin is a costume designer, educator, and author who heads the Costume Design program at the University of California, Irvine. She is President of the University/Resident Theater Association (URTA) and actively works to bridge students to professional training programs and early career opportunities. She is the co-author of *The Designs of Ann Roth* and *The Art and Practice of Costume Design* and has authored five articles for the journal *Theater Design & Technology*. She recently designed the costumes for The Shakespeare Center of Los Angeles's production of *Henry IV, Parts 1 and 2*, starring Tom Hanks as Falstaff and Joe Morton as King Henry. Other costume designs include regional theatres such as South Coast Repertory, PlayMakers Theater, Cincinnati Playhouse, New York Theater Workshop, the Mint Theater, Actors' Gang, Geffen Playhouse, Mark Taper Forum, Repertory Theater of St. Louis, and Portland Center Stage. International designs include the *Arezzo Festival* in Italy, Chekhov's *The Wood Demon* in London, the UK tour of *Miss Evers' Boys*, *Don Juan Flamenco* in Spain, and Baroque opera costume construction in Germany. Website: www.hollypoedurbin.com.

Christin Essin, Third Editor and Writer

Essin is Associate Professor of Theatre History at Vanderbilt University in Nashville, Tennessee. She has published numerous essays on theatre design artistry, technology, and backstage labor in publications such as *Theatre Journal*, *Theatre Topics*, and *Theatre History Studies*. Her first book, *Stage Designers in Early Twentieth Century America* (2012), won a Golden Pen Award from the United States Institute for Theatre Technology. She is currently writing her second book, a cultural history and ethnography of unionized technicians in the International Alliance of Theatrical Stage Employees who work in New York City's commercial theatre industry. Before committing her career to teaching and scholarship, she worked professionally as a theatre electrician, lighting designer, and storyteller.

CONTRIBUTORS

Ashley Bellet

Bellet is a PhD candidate in the Interdisciplinary Theatre Studies Program at the University of Wisconsin–Madison. She holds BAs in English and Theatre Design from the University of the South at Sewanee and an MFA in Costume and Scenic Design from the University of Memphis. She is a professional costume designer and craftsperson and has designed and taught previously at the University of Memphis, Oklahoma City University, Millikin University, the University of Wisconsin–Madison, and the University of Tulsa. She has worked as a costume crafts artisan at American Players Theatre and the Santa Fe Opera and has designed for the Potsdam Music Theatre, Light Opera Oklahoma, Oklahoma City Repertory Theatre, the Kentucky Repertory Theatre, Theatre Tulsa, Theatre Memphis, and Playhouse on the Square, among others. Her research interests include postdramatic theatre aesthetics, material culture studies, and visual expressions of posthumanism on stage. Bellet has presented her research and pedagogical approaches to teaching design at the Association for Theatre in Higher Education (ATHE), American Alliance for Theatre Education (AATE), the United States Institute for Theatre Technology (USITT), and the Kennedy Center American College Theatre Festival (KCACTF). She is the Commissioner of Education and a member of the Board of Directors for the USITT, Associate Editor for Education for *Theatre Design & Technology*, and is currently the Wisconsin State Chair for KCACTF.

Erin Carignan

Carignan is a versatile costume designer who has worked in regional theatre, opera, dance, music videos, and print ads in roles ranging from costume designer, stylist, and textile artist to crafts artisan. She has been a part of more than one hundred and fifty professional productions with several theatre companies, most notably the Old Globe Theatre, Los Angeles Opera, La Jolla Playhouse, and Pioneer Theatre. Her research centers around her most passionate subjects: costume design, textile surface modification, and pushing the boundaries of design and technology using digital mediums and interfaces. She is most interested where these subjects intersect in theatrical artistry and technical application. This research ties in with her own book *The Dye Book: Dyeing and Painting for the Entertainment Industry* (on contract with FOCAL Press, 2020). She is an active member and presenter for USITT and

USA829. Carignan is currently Visiting Assistant Professor of Theatre in Costume Design at Purdue University.

Jeannie Galioto

Galioto is the Head of Costume Design and Assistant Professor at Western Illinois University. She has an MFA in Costume Design and has been a freelance costume designer and stylist for twenty-five years. She has worked all over the country and credits include productions for the San Diego Repertory Theatre, Diversionary Theatre (where she won an award for Best Costume Design), the Guthrie Lab, Crossroads Theater, Mixed Blood Theatre, Moxie Theatre, Youth Theatre Northwest, Park Square Theatre, and Shakespeare in the Park, to name a few. She has designed costumes for theatre, opera, dance, commercials, film, and music videos. She was an invited speaker at the Costume Colloquium in Florence, Italy, and she was the costume design assistant to Paul Tazewell for the multiple Tony Award–winning show *Memphis*. In addition to freelance designing, she has taught at The Art Institute, University of San Diego, San Diego State University, University of California, Irvine, The Fashion Institute of Design and Merchandising, City College, and Palomar College. Galioto has also worked with the Costume Design graduate program at the University of California San Diego as an advisor and mentor. She has worked for many years at the La Jolla Playhouse in La Jolla, California, and on numerous Broadway tours as a design assistant, an assistant shop manager, and a lead costume crafts artisan. She also helped to develop the Green Theater Choices Toolkit in conjunction with Mo'Olelo Performing Arts Company. Website: www.jeanniegalioto.com.

Jessica Hansen

Hansen is an award-winning Los Angeles–based costume designer and technician, with experience in theatre, dance, film, television, commercials, theme parks, and corporate clients. She has worked in costume design and construction for Disneyland Resort, Walt Disney World, Tide, Girl Scouts of America, Kaiser Permanente Educational Theater, Garry Marshall Theatre, The Lyric Theatre, South Coast Repertory, The Met Theater, Greenway Court Theater, San Juan Capistrano Shakespeare Festival, Stonebound Productions, and Poptent, among others. Hansen is a member of IATSE Local 829, United Scenic Artists in Costume Design. She received an MFA in Costume Design from the University of California, Irvine and a BFA in Costume Design and Technology from Emerson College. She is a published author, and her work has been featured in numerous theatre journals and books. She is an honored recipient of the Herbert D. Greggs Merit Award for an article published in the Winter 2018 edition of *Theatre Design & Technology Journal* by USITT. Her work is published in *The Art and Practice of Costume Design*, *Showcase*, *Developing and Maintaining a Design-Tech Portfolio*, and USITT's *Theatre Design & Technology Journal*. Hansen is proud to be the head faculty and creator of the costume program at East Los Angeles College in the Theatre Arts Department.

Martha A. Marking

Marking is Professor of Costume and Makeup Design and Technology at Appalachian State University in Boone, North Carolina. Originally from Madison, Wisconsin, her professional credits include design/technology work at the Utah Shakespearean Festival, Wisconsin

Shakespeare Festival, Illinois Shakespeare Festival, Wake Forest University, the University of Hawaii–Manoa, the University of North Carolina–Greensboro, and the Blowing Rock Stage Company. At Appalachian State some of her more than eighty design credits include *A Midsummer Night's Dream*, *Radium Girls*, *Love's Labour's Lost*, *Misalliance*, *Tartuffe*, *The Diary of Anne Frank*, *Big Love*, *Avenue Q*, and *Twelfth Night*. Marking has also done custom knitwear for the University of North Carolina School of the Arts productions of *Angels in America Part 1: Millennium Approaches* and *Stage Door*. She has served several terms as a member of the board of directors of USITT and was most recently the Vice-President for Members, Sections and Chapters. She was Chair of the USITT Southeast Section for five years. Marking was a co-editor of USITT's *Projects for Teaching Costume Design and Technology, Vol. 2*, and has several projects published in that edition. She is a frequent book reviewer for *Theatre Design & Technology* and wrote "Chain Mail Techniques from the Utah Shakespearean Festival" and "A Costume Facilities Checklist," also published in *Theatre Design & Technology*.

Anthony R. Phelps

Phelps has taught for over twenty years at several universities, including Emerson College, the University of Kentucky, and Bradley University. While teaching, he has remained active as a freelance scenic and lighting designer and scenic artist. His work has been seen at North Shore Music Theatre, the Nora Theatre, Boston Playwright's Theatre, Boston Children's Theatre, New England Conservatory, Providence Black Rep, Central City Opera, and Theatre L'Homme Dieu. His film and television credits as a scenic artist include *Castle Rock*, *Knives Out*, *The Equalizer*, *Grown Ups 2*, *Here Comes the Boom*, *That's My Boy*, and *Tell Me a Story*. He is a member of United Scenic Artists and IATSE. Phelps has been an active member of the USITT since 1996. He has also held several positions in the national organization, including Lighting Commissioner; Vice-Commissioner for Scenic Art; Vice-Commissioner for Programming: Lighting Commission; and Paint Lab Coordinator.

Rachel E. Pollock

Pollock has worked as a professional costume craftsperson for theatre, opera, ballet, television, and film since 1994. After freelancing in Knoxville, Chicago, and Boston, she accepted a staff position as resident Lead Crafts Artisan and Dyer for the American Repertory Theatre at Harvard University in Cambridge, where she served for four award-winning seasons. She subsequently relocated to Los Angeles to work in film and television costuming as well as a stint on the crafts team of the LA Opera before relocating to Chapel Hill, North Carolina. She has served as a crafts artisan, dyer, and milliner for such designers as Catherine Zuber, Ann Hould-Ward, William Ivey Long, Gregg Barnes, Constance Hoffman, and Julie Taymor, and worked for Parsons-Meares, LTD on Tim Hatley's Tony Award–winning costume designs for *Shrek the Musical*. Pollock is the author of *Sticks in Petticoats*, the only extant text on parasol history and construction for the stage, as well as various articles for trade publications such as the *Costume Research Journal*. She maintains the seminal costume crafts artisanship blog, La Bricoleuse. At UNC, she conducts a series of graduate seminars on costume craftwork—millinery, dyeing and distressing, masks, armor, and related topics.

Leah Ramillano
Ramillano is a CAD III Associate Draftsperson for Mattel's Tradeshow Services Department as well as a freelance scenic designer based in southern California. She is an alumnus of the Oregon Shakespeare Festival's FAIR Program and co-founder of the Women+ In Theatre group. Ramillano values the practice of aligning your integrity as an artist with your integrity as a human being, and understanding that the work of the theatre extends beyond the stage. She is an advocate for the intersectionality of oppressed identities and the importance of collaboration to tell those stories. She holds her MFA in Scenic Design from the University of California, Irvine where she designed *The Liquid Plain*, *These Shining Lives*, and *Parade*. Recent design credits include *Seussical*, *Comb Your Hair (Or You'll Look Like a Slave)*, and *The Wizard of Oz*. Website: leahramillano.com.

Courtney Smith
Smith is a scenic and media designer for live performance. He works primarily in theatre, dance, and film but can also be found working on music videos, corporate window displays, events, and anything with a solid story and a great group of people behind it. Smith's designs have received several Meritorious Achievement Awards from the Kennedy Center American College Theatre Festival. Additionally, his work received a Distinguished Achievement Award in Scenic Design from the Kennedy Center in Washington, DC. Credits include the Warren Miller Performing Arts Center, Southwark Playhouse, the Bushwick Starr, Roundabout Theatre Company, New York City Opera, Playwrights Horizons, Classic Stage Company, Cedar Lake Dance, Marvel Repertory Theatre, Mount Baker Repertory Theatre, Montana Shakespeare in the Parks, Coeur d'Alene Summer Theatre, and Idaho Repertory Theatre. Smith is a member of USITT and has an MFA in Scenic Design from the University of Idaho. In addition, he serves as Vice-Chair of Design, Technology & Management for the Kennedy Center American College Theatre Festival (KCACTF) in Region VII. Most importantly, he is the proud father of son Brayden and daughter Harper.

Leslie Stamoolis
Stamoolis is Assistant Professor of Theater and Dance at Gonzaga University. At Gonzaga, she has designed and built costumes for, among others, *Jesus Christ Superstar*, *Much Ado About Nothing*, *Troilus and Cressida*, and *Mr. Burns, a Post-Electric Play*. She also produced/directed Gonzaga's first public performance of *The Vagina Monologues*. She has served as a costume technician for Marriott Theatre of Lincolnshire and Kaiser Permanente Educational Theatre and as the Director of Education for Cincinnati Shakespeare Company. As a researcher, her focus is in finding eco-friendly and sustainable practices in costume design and construction. In 2017, her study of natural versus synthetic dyes was presented at the USITT Annual Conference's adjudicated Tech Expo; it was named one of the top five projects and her abstract was published in USITT's quarterly journal,

Theatre Design & Technology. In 2019, she led a panel on parenthood in theatre at the USITT Annual Conference. Stamoolis holds an MA in Theatre from Miami University and an MFA in Costume Design from the University of California, Irvine.

Skye Strauss

Strauss is currently pursuing an Interdisciplinary PhD in Theatre and Drama at Northwestern University. Her dissertation explores how performing objects participate in collective creation and foster intense affective experiences for audience members. Her research uses puppetry theory and new materialism to justify framing these assertive objects as collaborators. Her case studies span theatre, contemporary circus, and dance. In the classroom, Strauss is currently teaching a History of European Theatrical Design & Technology. She is always looking for new ways to combine practice and research with her students. Her writing has been presented in the Puppetry and Material Performance working group at the American Society for Theatre Research (ASTR) and a panel presentation called "Costume and Meaning Making in Circus Performance" at the Association for Theatre in Higher Education (ATHE). Her publications include a performance review in *Puppetry International* and a book review in *Theatre Topics*. Strauss is currently exploring what it means to dramaturg for designers, for instance, serving as a "costume researcher" for Linda Roethke's design for *Visiting Edna* at Steppenwolf. Prior to coming to Northwestern, Strauss worked as a professional costume designer and technician at theatres throughout the city of Chicago including the Piven Theatre Workshop and the Chicago Shakespeare Theater. She earned her BA in Theatre with University Honors at the University of Alabama at Birmingham and her MA in Drama and Performance Studies from Queen's University Belfast (Northern Ireland) as a Rotary Scholar. When she is not on campus, she can be found building magical things or hanging upside-down at the circus.

Michael Vincent

Vincent is the Costume Shop Manager for the University of Massachusetts Boston Performing Arts Department. He graduated from the University of Massachusetts Boston in 2016 with a BA, summa cum laude. He has since worked with UMass Boston's excellent performing arts department to produce several plays and theatrical performances, and continues to enjoy working with the wide variety of students, and amazing talents, at the school. As the oldest child of a family of five children, theatre has long been a part of Vincent's life, starting in the third grade when he starred in the local high school's holiday performance, playing a rock n' roll snowman out to save the town. He would go on to teach theatre for the Homeschool Association of Middle Georgia, teaching homeschooled kids the wonderful attributes of theatre, and to create a small traveling theatrical company that produced and performed plays in Georgia to increase the awareness of the power of the stage and to encourage everyone to spread their wings and experience theatre for the first time, whether acting in a performance or seeing their first show. The inspirational power of the theatre for all is a philosophy that Vincent holds dearly to this day and hopes to instill in the students that he currently is working with.

Amber Voner

Voner is a Boston-based hair and wig designer/technician for theatre and film. Her professional credits include *Little Women* (Columbia Pictures), *Jagged Little Pill*, *Waitress: The Musical*, *Porgy and Bess* (American Repertory Theater), *Sleeping Beauty*, and *The Nutcracker* (Boston Ballet). Voner has also designed for Emerson Stage, the Lyric Stage Company, Actors' Shakespeare Project, and Company One. She received her BFA in Theatre Design and Technology from Emerson College, is passionate about "Green Beauty," and teaches makeup artistry and wig styling and maintenance workshops at UMass Boston and Emerson College. Website: ambervoner.com.

INDEX